CHRISTIAN

The Heart of The Matter

A Concise Guide

David Evans

Tahilla Press

Eastbourne

ISBN 978-1-907228-08-7

Published by Tahilla Press
e-mail: tahillapress@tahilla.com

Acknowledgments

I would like to thank the Lord for inspiring me and sustaining me throughout the writing of this book, while I have juggled with other commitments. Thanks also to my wife Yvonne for her patience and encouragement and being the first person to read and critique my manuscript.

I would also like to thank: Charles and Rachel Claydon for the use of their wonderful retreat 'The Hiding Place' and Alan and Polly Bootle for the use of their caravan, my mother-in-law Mavis for the use of her home, and Paul and Jane Hames for letting me stay with them and write in their lovely home in Gilo, Jerusalem. Brian Niblock and David Hind, the former and current Senior Pastors of my church, for their encouragements and help. John Sim, Jez Smith, Yoel Seaton, Steve Vickers, Gary Norton and Mike Reeves deserve a mention for reviewing my manuscripts and offering invaluable constructive criticism.

I am grateful to Dave Roberts of Tahilla Press for his help and advice on publishing and distribution.

Gratitude is also due to my local friends, too numerous to mention, who have constantly encouraged me to stick at the task.

Contact details

Anyone who wishes to contact me with questions about and/or criticisms of this book is welcome to do so:

David Evans
Email: theheartofthematter@hotmail.co.uk

Contents

Prologue

A popular Evangelical Anglican church in the UK was looking for a new Vicar. Someone who attends the church said that each of the church's Home Groups had been asked to list some points that they see as desirable in their church's new leader. One of hers was that he should love Israel - But the group leader refused to add that to the list for the reason that he saw it as too trivial!

The attitude displayed by that group leader is all too typical of many UK Christians. I hope, with this book, to show you that the issues surrounding Israel are far from trivial. If they *are* trivial, how come there is such a worldwide furore about Israel?

Stephen Sizer, in one of his books, says *'a large proportion of Bible-believing Christians are convinced that God blesses those nations that stand with Israel and curses those that don't.'* [1] That may be the case in the USA and certain other nations, but not so much here in the UK. The situation here is more correctly reflected by Walter Riggans who points out that *'there have always been Christians whose reading of the Bible convinced them of God's continuing purposes for his "ancient people", but they have always been a minority, sometimes marginalised by the mainstream church leaderships'* [2]

I have over 200 very useful books on Israel, Palestine, Judaism and the Jewish roots of Christianity. The Amazon website also lists some 8000 books on the subject of all shades of opinion. Why another book? Well, I just feel that a shorter book is needed as an introduction and one which does not ignore opposing points of view.

My aim is to write an introductory book for Christians and to keep it as short as possible, even at the risk of not being able to back up my arguments sufficiently. This book is aimed mainly at Christians who fall into two categories. One category are those who have not looked into the issues. The other is those who have but have not yet come to any real conclusion. Hopefully, this introductory survey will tempt the reader to do some further study and I list other books and resources that go into more detail.

This book is written out of a strong desire to build a bridge of understanding with some of my fellow Christians who, for various reasons, do not see things my way. My own journey of understanding so far has been a long one and a radical turnaround from ideas I held to earlier in my Christian life. I am sympathetic to the struggles of believers who find it difficult to come to terms with some of the issues and are confused by different interpretations of the Bible. Meeting other Christians who seem to look at Israel through 'rosy-tinted spectacles' has not helped some Christians.

I was brought up in an Evangelical Christian environment, which said nothing about the modern State of Israel and the reasons why, against massive odds, the Jews, have survived as a people to this day. After my own personal coming to faith in 1972, I spent some years in charismatic churches where it was taught that the church had *replaced* Israel and that God's purposes with the Jews *as a nation* ended in the first century AD.

In 1985, I commenced a systematic and consecutive reading of the 'Old' Testament with no agenda other than to become more familiar with it. I got a lot more than I bargained for as I was confronted on page after page with God's dealings with and promises to Israel.

I once had a conversation with a British Pastor who had formerly believed that Israel still had a distinct and special place in the purposes of God but had more recently changed his mind. He claimed that God had said to him that he would never have come to his earlier understanding from the scriptures alone, but only by what others had taught him. That's ironic because my own understanding *did* come from reading the scriptures alone. Only in later years did I learn from other people on the subject.

I remember a pastor's son who lodged in my home for a year who had been brought up, in contrast to me, to believe that the Jews were still a special, chosen people. It was all he had known on the subject and he was questioning it. Fair enough, I say- we need to be sure about what God's Word says, whatever the traditions we grew up with.

There is a strange kind of logic, or lack of logic, behind a lot of what goes on between Israel and the surrounding nations. This is illustrated by a joke, which I hesitate to introduce as a lot of what happens with respect to Israel is simply not funny. However, in the interests of some light relief on a heavy subject, I include it as it is written in a particular book.

'One of the most popular stories in Israel is the one about a fish which was asked by a scorpion to take him on his back across the Jordan River. At first the fish refused. "You would", he said, "sting me". "Why would I?" replied the scorpion. "You know I can't swim. If I stung you, I too would drown." So, the fish saw the point and agreed to carry the scorpion, but halfway across the scorpion stung him. "You fool," said the fish, "now we will both drown. Why did you do that?" "Oh, I don't know", replied the scorpion; "this is the Middle East!"' [3]

I am grateful to a new Christian friend and fellow visitor I met in Israel in 2007, Darren Woodward from New Zealand, for introducing me to the expression *'doubt is the handmaiden of truth.'* I hope that those who up to now see things differently from me will allow doubt to spur them on to re-examine God's word.

Some issues I touch on in this book are:

- The need to have a scriptural foundation to our views
- Media misrepresentation of the Israel/Palestine issues

- God's covenants with Israel
- The Jewish return to the Land of Israel
- Islam and Israel
- Our British 'Christian Zionist' heritage
- The wider purposes of God through Israel

The principles I discuss in chapter 7 are of particular importance. *It has always been in God's heart that Israel should bless the other nations and have the widest possible impact on them.*
 You may end up saying that you still disagree with the perspective I present in some ways. Even still, I hope that you will still have a better understanding of what those who enthuse about present-day Israel actually believe. There has been much misrepresentation of us. To some extent, that may be our fault for not explaining ourselves properly!

  The Senior Pastor of my church in Leicester and my good friend and fellow elder, David Hind, in his book 'In Hindsight', complains that most Christian books are too long. I have kept this book as short as I can while including the themes most crucial to an understanding of what lies at 'The Heart of the Matter.'

  Finally, a word from ancient history- Thycydides, a fifth century Greek historian said *'most people will not take pains to get at the truth of things, and are much more inclined to accept the first story they hear'.*

NOTES

1. *Zion's Christian Soldiers*, p 7, Inter-Varsity Press 2007.
2. *The Covenant with the Jews*, p 58, Monarch Publications 1992.
3. *Israel Today* by Richard Wolff p 7, Tyndale House Publishers 1970.

It may be that, by the time you read this book, some of the Internet links quoted will be unavailable. As you will appreciate, that is beyond my control.

Introduction

I should first of all point out that this book assumes that the reader accepts the Bible as the authoritative, revealed Word of God. However, I recognise that differences exist in some areas of interpretation.

I do realise that some confusion can arise in the use of the word 'Israel'. In this book, I use the word almost always in two ways. One is simply the Jewish people in a biblical and historical sense- you could say 'ethnic Israel'. The other is the modern state of Israel, founded in 1948. I cannot define my use in every instance and so I leave it to the reader to judge by the context.

When I first began to read the 'Old' Testament properly, I was strongly impressed by the sheer volume of material about Israel and the Jews. In light of this, (plus the fact that much of the New Testament is set in Israel), the prevailing apathy amongst western Christians about Israel is truly astonishing. It is even more surprising in light of the events of the twentieth century.

The Jerusalem based Bible teacher Lance Lambert travels all over the world. He says that everywhere else *but* here in the West believers just read the Bible and come to the understanding that Israel still has a special place in God's purposes.

You are hopefully reading this chapter because something in the Prologue got you interested enough to carry on reading. What I need to do now is to tell you *why* I believe the ground I cover in this book is so important. Some of my Christian friends are baffled by the amount of time and energy I put into this area. I'm sure that they sometimes must think that I am majoring on minors, but are too polite to say.

Throughout this book I use the term *'Christian Zionist'* as a loose term of reference to Christians of a broadly similar persuasion to my own. I am not entirely happy with the term, which seems to have been popularised by our opponents and is often used in a derogatory way. However, a term of reference is needed so it will have to do. I do not claim to speak for all Christian Zionists on every point and I must bear responsibility for my own views.

Am I pro-Israeli or pro-Palestinian? The simple answer is I am pro-God, pro the Bible and pro all people. And pro getting the facts! On the one hand, the Bible says a lot about the return of the Jews to Israel. On the other, justice is an important biblical theme. I have compassion for the Palestinians and their problems, but there is a Palestinian propaganda machine to take into account. The Jews too are capable of propaganda and terrorism. Chapter 5 outlines some of the key points connected with the Israel/Palestine conflict.

I don't necessarily have a problem with pro-Palestinian groups unless they insist on putting the blame for all of the problems of the Palestinians on Israel. Some of them seem to me to do that. The Western world is obsessed with 'human rights' and 'equal rights' and this has no doubt rubbed off on many Christians as they look at the situation with Israel and the surrounding nations. I hope that this book will give you fresh insights.

I use certain terms in this book that will be unfamiliar to some readers and the glossary towards the end should be consulted.

Here is an outline of some of the issues and questions that I feel are important.

God is a Covenant-keeper
Much of it has to do with the covenant-keeping nature of God. *When is a promise not a promise?* The Bible contains various covenants God has made with man, and some of are actually *unconditional.* Terms like 'everlasting' and 'to all generations' are used, although the exact meanings of the Greek and Hebrew words translated in that way are debated. Can we really say

14

today that only the New Covenant is of any significance and dismiss the earlier ones by saying that all things are now 'fulfilled in Christ'?

Chapter 2 looks into the issue of God's covenants.

God's honour is at stake!
If God has not kept His promises to the Jews, will He keep His promises to the church and to individual Christians? What if *we* are unfaithful, as Israel has been? One Jewish pastor once said 'if God has not been true to the Jew, He may not be true to *you*'!

Is the whole Bible true?
And then, there's our attitude to the Bible. We say that we accept all 66 books as the inspired, authoritative Word of God- but *do* we? Dividing it into two parts and calling the first one the 'Old' Testament doesn't back up our claim.

The well-known Messianic Jewish singer Helen Shapiro, when she was searching for God, went into a Jewish bookshop asking for an 'Old' Testament. *'How* old?' asked the owner, with typical Jewish dry humour.

Do you realise that when Paul says that *'all scripture is given by inspiration of God and is profitable for doctrine, for reproof, for correction, for instruction in righteousness…'*[1] that he was *not* referring to the New Testament, which as such did not exist at the time the epistle was written?

Some Christians today say that they *do* believe the whole Bible, but its just that they let the New Testament interpret the 'Old'. This sounds good on the face of it but, if you look into it carefully enough, you will see that it can be a cover-up for minimising or even denying certain parts of the 'Old' Testament.

Where on earth do we start?
I suggest not with the media and/or books written by well-meaning Christians about peace and justice and reconciliation. Such books have their place but *sometimes* evidence a lack of understanding of some of the core issues at stake in the Israel/Palestine conflict.

So, where does a Christian start with unravelling all this? *Unsurprisingly, the answer is with the scriptures*, without underestimating the difficulties of applying them to current events as they actually unfold in and around Israel.

I have found, in conversation with some Christians who are not well up on Israel that, when you bring the prophetic passages into it, they want to sidestep them and jump straight to their understanding of fairness and justice. There are, of course, questions needing to be addressed in that area, but how do you avoid getting lost in a fog of human opinions? Studying the scriptures relevant to Israel requires time and patience.

Particularly in the earlier chapters of this book, I refer to many passages of scripture. The references are there for those who want to look into the context.

Why bother with Bible Prophecy?
Some Christians don't think we should spend time on the details of prophetic passages in the Bible. The reasons given are that it is too controversial and isn't very practical. *But* as one Bible teacher once pointed out, about a quarter of the content of the Bible relates to predictive prophecy and to ignore it would mean that he would be only doing three-quarters of his job!

Some highly-significant prophecies appear to have been fulfilled in, or not long before, our lifetimes, so it can't be said that the subject is not a practical one. More could of course be fulfilled in the near future.

Bible Interpretation

Some important questions have to be asked, for example:

- How literal or otherwise should one's approach to Bible interpretation be?
- Was a certain prophecy fulfilled in the past, is its fulfilment in the future, or could there be elements of both?
- Does 'Israel' in the Bible sometimes stand for the church, or not?

This may seem like hard work and it is tempting to leave it to others, such as pastors and Bible college students and the specialists in the field. It may be difficult at first to see why it is so important. After all, it doesn't affect our salvation. Well, the events in the Middle East aren't going to go away and they will increasingly affect the rest of the world.

Anti-semitism in the church

By 'anti-semitism', I mean 'anti-Jewish' (see Glossary). Several things in particular have combined to produce in the church, generally speaking, an anti-Jewish prejudice. This is sometimes only latent but, at other times, virulent and active.

These things are:

- An insufficient biblical understanding on Israel on the part of Christians today
- Deep historical roots of the anti-semitism that arose in the church of the first and second centuries after a rift between the Jewish and Gentile elements developed. This has persisted over the centuries ever since.
- The influence of the secular media on believers, who watch more TV than they spend time reading the Bible

God said to Abraham *'those who bless thee I will bless and those who curse thee I will curse'* [2]. Yes, the meaning of the descendants of Abraham extends to include the descendants of Ishmael and *spiritual* descendants and I am *not* saying that anyone who questions Christian Zionism is automatically cursing the Jews. But do you want to be blessed and your church and nation likewise?

Something called 'Replacement Theology' has grown up in the church and I deal with this in chapters 2 and 3.

Would a *'Palestinian'* State be an *'Islamic'* State?

The writers of certain Christian books, some of which contain very valid points about Israeli misdeeds and about biblical justice, often fail to deal adequately with the issue of Islam and Israel. They do not point out Islamic territorial ambitions. There is a fundamental requirement in radical Islam to take back for Islam areas of land that were once under Islamic control, but are no longer. Some people passionately advocate the creation of a Palestinian State, supposedly to exist peacefully alongside Israel.

Could they be unwittingly falling in line with an Islamic agenda which is part of something much bigger than they realise? I outline my thoughts on this in chapter 5.

Doubting leaders

I am generalising, as there are notable exceptions to this trend, but there has been an about turn by our national Christian leadership. To read some of the opponents of Christian Zionism, you would think that we had invented completely new ideas! In fact, our beliefs are broadly in line with the views of large numbers of British Christian leaders of earlier times, some of whom are very famous names.

They affirmed God's plans for the Jews when little progress, if any, could actually be seen. On the other hand, many modern British Christian leaders seem to deny the significance

18

of what is happening right under their noses. Chapter 6 is essential reading on the background of 'Britain and Israel'.

Missing the boat?
If Christian Zionists are right, there is something very critical going on in Israel and Palestine and much yet to come. All this, we believe, has a crucial inter-relation with God's dealings with the church, the other nations, Islam, and the Second Coming of our Lord. What a shame it would be to miss out on such an exciting time in human history through ignorance or false teaching.

An unhelpful feature of 'anti Christian Zionist literature' is a tendency, deliberate or otherwise, to tar all Christian Zionists and Christian Zionist organisations with the same brush. There is, in fact, considerable diversity in belief and emphasis as well as a common core among us.

Some common misrepresentations of our beliefs are:

- We all believe Israel can do no wrong
- We believe Jews do not need Jesus for salvation
- We believe that Christians who reject Christian Zionism will lose their salvation
- We are anti-Arab

See Appendix 1 for clarification on this.

The challenge
Some Christians set aside the issue of Israel because they find the concept of a renewal of God's dealing with Israel as a nation hard to reconcile with certain parts of the Bible, especially in the New Testament. However, do we reject or neglect, for example, the idea of the afterlife because there are passages that we find hard to reconcile?

It is time-consuming and challenging to think it all through, but very rewarding. I personally won't settle for anything less than the fullest insights God is willing to give me. Yes, we'll never understand it all, but we live in awesome days. Let's press on to know more of what our God is doing.

To those who decry Christian Zionism, I would point to the words of Rabbi Gamaliel in Acts '...*if their purpose or activity is of human origin, it will fail. But if it is from God, you will not be able to stop these men; you will only find yourselves fighting against God.'*[3]

It is important that Christian Zionists remain Jesus-centred rather than Israel-centred, even when it is our ministry to emphasise what God is doing with and through Israel. We talk a lot about the Land of Israel, but not because we think that the land is more important than the salvation of the Jews and the Gentiles. Having said that, the Bible is not ethereal- it is a book rooted in the real earth and real events on the earth. The happenings unfolding in Israel form an essential backdrop to the final salvation plans of God, as explained in this book.

My first and shortest chapter is called "The 'Either/Or' Mentality' of the Church". This may seem a strange title but it gives an important background of understanding to the following chapters.

NOTES

1. 2 Timothy 3 vs 16 (KJV)
2. Genesis 12 vs 3 (KJV)
3. Acts 5:38 & 39

Recommended introductory books for further reading:
1. *Land of Many Names* by Steve Maltz
2. *Understanding Israel* by Malcolm Hedding

Chapter 1

The 'Either/Or' Mentality of the Church

Christians often seem to feel they must choose between two seeming opposites on a point of doctrine, rather than embrace both aspects. I can understand it, as sometimes the opposite sides of the argument seem contradictory and irreconcilable.

I will give some examples of this tendency to polarise and then explain the relevance of the point to this book:

- *Law or Grace*- Is the 'Old' Testament *all law* and the New Testament *all grace*, or is there some of each in *both* Testaments?

- *Predestination or Freewill*- Did God *choose us*, or did we *choose Him*, or is it *both*?

- Do we seek to meet the material needs of people, which some call a 'social gospel', or preach the gospel to them? Why not both, as opportunities arise?

- With regard to Bible prophecies, is the fulfilment *literal or spiritual*, or *both*? Can a prophecy have *more than one* fulfilment at different times, or does it have to be *just one*? One Bible teacher has said that Bible prophecy is pattern with ultimate fulfilment.

- For example, link 2 Thessalonians 2:7 and 8- *'the secret power of lawlessness is already at work...and then the lawless one will be revealed'*. Is there the spirit of Antichrist in *every* generation, *or* is there a man who at the end of time will be revealed as The Antichrist? Or is it *both*?

- Has the Kingdom of God *already come* on earth- or is it *yet to come* in the future, or is it *both*? Should we focus on an *earthly* Jerusalem, or a *heavenly* Jerusalem, or *both*? (In any case, the *heavenly* Jerusalem will become an *earthly* one in the end- see Revelation 21)

- With respect to the Sabbath, should we keep one day a week as a *special day* of rest, or just seek to live in the sabbath rest of Jesus *every day*? Again could it be *both*?

- Some Christians say that we should only confess our sins to God. Others say we can also confess to each other. Who is right? Both positions are in the New Testament.

The fact of the matter is that, in the Bible, there is support for *all* of the positions I have just mentioned. I am sure a lot of arguments and pain and division could have been avoided in the church over the centuries, were it not for this tendency we have to polarise.

Relevance to Israel issues
For my part, I as a Christian Zionist, need to avoid polarisation when it comes to the place of the Arabs in God's purposes. As Canon Andrew White of Baghdad has said *'Churches either ignore the Palestinians and just take the side of the Israelis, or just take the side of Palestinians and ignore the other. Both are in need and both have rights'.*[1]

Could this unnecessary polarisation be part of the problem some Christians have when it comes to considering the role of Israel in God's end time plans? So, it *used to be* the Jews, but once the church came on the scene then of course it has to be *only* the church!

In chapter 3, I deal with a point about interpretation of the phrase 'Seed of Abraham'. Many Christians, for some reason, seem to feel it can only have one meaning, and that is the 'spiritual' descendants of Abraham, the church. I have pointed out that the expression has three meanings in the New Testament.

Paul Libermann says *'Some church leaders say the prophecies concerning Israel are for spiritual Israel (the church). Other Jewish scholars argue that these prophecies are for the descendants of Jacob. Actually, both positions are correct and they do not contradict one another'.*[2]

Genesis 12:1-3 contains the promises to Abraham and we can easily limit our understanding of those promises. Chuck Cohen points out that *"God's initial promise to Father Abraham is not an 'a la carte' restaurant menu where you can choose one item but reject another." Either it is all true or none of it'.*[3] He goes on to say that the promise contains a land, a great nation, a great name/reputation (Abraham), blessings and curses, *and* the gospel to the Gentiles.

Some Christians are simplistic when it comes to looking at the reasons why many of the Jews of the first century rejected Jesus. Of course, Jesus came not to set up an *earthly* kingdom, but a *spiritual* one they say, and if only those Jews had realised it. The fact is that Jesus set up the spiritual one first and is yet to set up the earthly one. Timing is the issue and this is at the root of a common misunderstanding about Acts chapter 1 and the restoration of the kingdom to Israel (see Chapter 3).

And the issue of the Jews returning to the Land of Israel - was everything fulfilled in the return from Babylon? Or did some prophecies remain to be fulfilled until a return from the worldwide scattering? Why *either/or-* Why not *both*?

We will look in the next chapter at God's covenants with Israel.

NOTES

1. *Christianity* magazine, June 2009, page 19.
2. *The Fig Tree Blossoms*, p 69, Paul Liberman, Fountain Press, ISBN 0-89350-000-3.
3. *Sword* magazine, March/April 2007, page 11.

Chapter 2

Has God Finished with Israel?

When I pose the question 'Has God finished with Israel'?, I am thinking of them as a people or race. It is obviously open to individual Jews to come to faith in Christ.

Common Ground
All Bible-believing Christians accept that God did choose Israel in the first place. His purpose in doing so is expressed in Exodus when God told Moses to tell the Israelites *'now if you obey me fully and keep my covenant, then out of all nations you will be my treasured possession. Although the whole earth is mine, you will be for me a kingdom of priests and a holy nation'.* [1]

We have in the Bible highlights of Israel's history up to the first century AD and, as we all know, apart from a holy remnant, they did not obey God fully in the ways He required. However, we need to be careful about the conclusions we draw from this. After all, we are warned in Romans 11:17-18 not to boast over the branches that have been temporarily broken off, that is the Jews.

Is the church's record of obedience any better than Israel's? By the time the letters to the seven churches described in the book of Revelation chapters 2 and 3 were written (most likely in around AD 95), the rot had already begun to set in. Books on church history paint a very mixed picture of the church's progress after those days.

Consequences of Israel's Disobedience
The 'million-dollar' question is what was the effect of Israel's disobedience on God's promises to them? Did God lose patience with them and start again with a second covenant people? This is where

Christians differ. Answers to that question vary between yes, no and ideas that are in between the two.

At one time, God *did* want to destroy the Israelites and he thought of starting again with Moses and his descendants. In Exodus we read '*I have seen these people*' the Lord said to Moses, '*and they are a stiff-necked people. Now leave me alone so that my anger may burn against them and that I may destroy them. Then I will make you into a great nation.*'[2] Moses talked the Lord out of it and, reading between the lines, he must have noticed what a great opportunity it would have been to make a name for himself. Instead, he reminded God of the promises He had sworn to Abraham, Isaac and Israel (Jacob) and '*the Lord relented*'.[2]

As the highlights of Israel's history in the Bible continue, more episodes of disobedience and idolatry follow with God visiting them with judgments and also with limited periods of restoration and prosperity and times of the Glory of God coming down.

In particular, a track record emerged of refusing to listen to prophets sent to them by the Lord, as graphically put by Stephen the Martyr in Acts …'*you are just like your fathers: 'You always resist the Holy Spirit! Was there ever a prophet your fathers did not persecute'?*[3]

Exiled from the Land

In 2 Kings we read that '*In the ninth year of Hoshea, the king of Assyria captured Samaria and deported the Israelites to Assyria*'…'*All this took place because the Israelites had sinned against the Lord their God…*'[4] This happened in the eighth century BC.

Again, in 2 Kings, it says '*in the ninth year of Zedekiah's reign…Nebuchadnezzar king of Babylon marched against Jerusalem with his whole army*'.[5] The chapter goes on to describe the destruction of the Temple by the Babylonians and that '*Judah went into captivity, away from her land*'.[6] This happened in the sixth century BC and the exile lasted 70 years as predicted by Jeremiah.[7]

In the days of King Rehoboam, son of Solomon, the twelve tribes of Israel split into two divisions, or kingdoms. Judah and Benjamin became known as the 'Jews' and the other ten as the 'Israelites'. Today, however, it is common to refer to the descendants of all 12 tribes as 'Jews', as I do in the main in this book.

Some Israelites had already left the Land before the Assyrian deportation. Others were able to return from time to time, meaning that there was still a representation of the Israelites in the Land. There was also a gradual return of the Jews after the Babylonian exile.

Part of God's judgments on the Jews is that they can be temporarily exiled from the Land of Israel, as set out in the closing chapters of Leviticus and of Deuteronomy. More on this later in this chapter and in chapter 4. For now, I make passing reference to exile to set the scene at the time of Jesus.

Post-Exile Israel

So, when the 'Old' Testament record is concluded, the Jews are still around despite blowing it time and time again! God had not abandoned them- at least at that point.

At the time of Jesus, many are still in the Land albeit under the rule of earth's most powerful empire of the time, Rome. Many others remained scattered throughout the other nations as we see from Acts 2:5-11.

By and large it is true to say that Israel *as a nation* rejected Jesus as Messiah and Saviour, even though many individual Jews did come to faith. However, much of the blame for the rejection lay with the Jewish establishment or leadership as we will see in chapter 3.

We now come to the real crunch question- what was the effect of the rejection of Jesus as Messiah? Was this the 'last straw' for the Lord? To find an answer we have to start with the 'Old' Testament.

27

God's Covenants

Christians have a misleading habit of referring to 'The Old Covenant' and 'The New Covenant' but what we actually find in the Bible is a *series* of covenants. In Jeremiah 31[8] we read of a New Covenant which is ...*'not like the covenant I made with their forefathers...'* The covenant made with their forefathers was the Mosiac, or legal, covenant given at Sinai. In Hebrews 8[9], the two covenants are compared and Jeremiah is quoted. However, there are *other covenants with Israel* not mentioned in these particular passages.

Those who try to use Hebrews 8 to prove that all the earlier covenants have been abolished and replaced by the New Covenant fail to differentiate between specific covenants, most of which are still in force.

The series of covenants to which I refer, and the representatives with whom they were made, can be summarised as follows:

- Adam[10]
  'Food' Covenant (My own term)
- Noah[11]
  No more universal floods
- Abraham, Isaac & Jacob[12]
  The Land
- Abraham[13]
  Circumcision
- Moses[14]
  Torah = Teaching or Instruction ('Law')
- Phineas[15]
  Perpetual Levitical Priesthood
- David[16]
  Throne to be established forever
- Israel & Judah[17]
  New Covenant

The nature of God's Covenants

We tend to think of a covenant as an agreement between two parties with binding conditions on both and, if either or both sides breaches the conditions, the covenant can be annulled. However, in Genesis 15:17-19, before God makes the covenant of the Land with Abram (later Abraham), in verse 18 we read, *'when the sun had set and darkness had fallen, a smoking brazier with a blazing torch appeared and passed between the pieces'.* The 'pieces' were the bodies of birds and animals cut in two (vs 9-10). Steve Maltz explains this very well.

'He made a covenant with Abram, in the custom and manner that such transactions were conducted in those days, except for one thing- only God signed the contract. Only God "passed between the pieces", which meant that only God had to fulfil the covenant conditions- the covenant was going to be unconditional, as far as Abram and his descendants were concerned. There would be no conditions for Abram to fulfil- or break.' [18]

It is the case, of course, that circumcision is the sign of that covenant.

By the time of Jesus, a Greek translation of the 'Old' Testament known as the Septuagint was in common use. In it, the Hebrew word for covenant *'berith'* is translated into Greek as *'diatheke'*. Fausset in his Bible Dictionary on page 140 says that *diatheke* means *'a gracious disposal by His own sovereign will'.* In the New Testament, the word translated as covenant is the word *diatheke* on every occasion. If the word *suntheke* had been used instead, the meaning would be *'a mutual compact'.*

Are all the Covenants unconditional?

The short answer is no, but there is only one that is conditional and that is the Mosaic one, the Law given at Sinai.

Consider as a point of principle the covenant with Noah, given to all life on the earth. There is no condition whatsoever made by God in the passage in Genesis 9. God sets His rainbow in the sky after the rain and there is nothing man or beast can do to hasten it or to hinder it. The sign of this covenant continues to the present day and the existence of the New Covenant hasn't changed it.

If you follow through the scripture references I have listed at the end of this chapter, you will see that no conditions are laid down for the various covenants, including the Land Covenant or even the New Covenant. The exception is the Mosaic Covenant, and if you go back to the passage I quoted at the beginning of this chapter, you will see the words *'if you obey me fully'*.

The Mosaic Covenant is the one in which the Israelites were given a part to play and a lot depends on their part. Deuteronomy 28 sets out the blessings for obedience to God's commandments and the curses for disobedience, one of which was to be exiled from the Land. Warnings about exile from the Land for disobedience are given[19], warnings which were repeated over and over again by the Prophets. Even a curse on the Land itself is pronounced.[20]

Does this mean that exile from the Land can be irreversible? We know that was not the case with the Babylonian exile, but that was before the Jews rejected Jesus.

God Himself is the *owner* of the Land, as of everywhere else on the earth, and He describes it in Joel as *'My Land'*.[21] However, He has chosen, for His own purposes, to give the Land to the physical descendants of Abraham, Isaac and Jacob to live in. Their residence in the Land was interrupted because the covenant with Moses was conditional and they were disobedient.

Promises of restoration to the Land are also given in Deuteronomy[22] and repeatedly confirmed in the books of the Prophets. So, residence can be suspended, but that doesn't change the covenant and the prospect of an eventual and a permanent return.

Some say that the promises of restoration to the Land were all fulfilled by the return from Babylon and I look at this theory in chapter 4.

Even though there were punishments for disobedience, the grace of God was still at work in Israel of old. It is the same in Israel today. Even though the Jews are returning largely in unbelief, God is blessing them and other nations with their medical and other scientific breakthroughs.

The passages in which the promises are made by God about the right to the Land often contain words like 'everlasting' and 'for ever'. This is a further indication of the permanence of the Land Covenant, although some argue that the Hebrew word 'olam' translated 'everlasting' or similar can mean a long period of time, but not something permanent.' My own view is that the Land Covenant is permanent, at least until the eternal age yet to come.

Conclusion about the Covenants

The majority are unconditional, and the one that is conditional comes with promises of restoration as well as promises of judgment. Therefore it can hardly be the case that God has finished with Israel. More in chapter 4 about exile from and restoration to the Land but, for now, let's stick with the question that is the title of this chapter.

Is there anything else in the 'Old' Testament that shows us unequivocally that God would never abandon His first covenant people, Israel? Yes, plenty, and I give just two examples below:

Chaos in the sky

Immediately following the passage in Jeremiah 31 about God making a New Covenant with the houses of Israel and Judah, there is a fascinating passage which is worth quoting in full:

'This what the LORD says, he who appoints the sun to shine by day, who decrees the moon and the stars to shine by night, who stirs up the sea so that its waves roar- the LORD Almighty is his name: "Only if these decrees vanish from my sight", declares the LORD, "will the descendants of Israel ever cease to be a nation before me". This is what the LORD says: "Only if the heavens above can be measured and the foundations of the earth below be searched out will I reject all the descendants of Israel because of all they have done" declares the LORD. [23]*

There is a similar passage in Jeremiah 33 and, at that time, people were saying *'The Lord has rejected the two kingdoms he chose'.* The Lord said *'So they despise my people and no longer regard them as a nation'.* [24] Unfortunately, much of the church has made a similar mistake.

The permanency of God's choice of Israel seems clear in the 'Old' Testament. If that is true, *nothing* can change that picture. However, some argue that the national rejection of Jesus by Israel *does* change the picture, and that there are other indications in the New Testament that God has rejected the Jews. This is considered in the next chapter.
As an aside, on a natural level, we might well ask the question as to why, if God washed his hands of the Jews in the first century, they have continued to make massive contributions to mankind in science, medicine, technology and many other areas. This is out of all proportion to their numbers compared to many other nations.

NOTES

1. Exodus 19: 5-6
2. Exodus 32: 9 & 14
3. Acts 7: 51-52.
4. 2 Kings 17: 6-7
5. 2 Kings 25: 1

32

6. 2 Kings 25: 21
7. Jeremiah 25: 11-12
8. Jeremiah 31: 31-34
9. Hebrews 8: 7-13
10. Genesis 1: 28-30
11. Genesis 9: 12-17
12. Genesis 12: 2-3; 13: 14-17; 15: 17-18; 17: 4-8; 26: 2-5; 28: 3-4.
13. Genesis 17: 9-14
14. Exodus 34: 27-28
15. Numbers 25: 10-13
16. 2 Samuel 7: 16 & 23: 5
17. Jeremiah 31: 31-34 & Hebrews 8: 8-13
18. *The Land of Many Names'* by Steve Maltz p 6, Authentic Lifestyle 2003.
19. Eg Deuteronomy 28:36-37
20. Eg Deuteronomy 29: 22-24.
21. Joel 3: 2
22. Deuteronomy 30: 1-10
23. Jeremiah 31: 35-37
24. Jeremiah 33: 24

Recommended books

Rob Richards 'Has God Finished with Israel?'
Derek Prince 'The Destiny of Israel and the Church'

(See list of Recommended Resources at back of book)

Chapter 3

The Rejection of Jesus

In chapter 2, we looked briefly at the question as to Israel's permanence from the 'Old' Testament point of view. We find evidence of permanence in scripture and there are many more passages in the 'Old' Testament we could have looked at. But *surely* the fact that the Jews rejected Jesus as Messiah and Saviour means that God's specific purposes with Israel as a people came to an end? After all, the promise of the Messiah is the greatest of all promises, designed to bring salvation blessings to every nation. And God brought in a new entity, the Church, as a covenant people from all nations.

Well, I would refer back to my comments in my introduction to this book under the heading 'Is the whole Bible true?' We have to harmonise different parts of the Bible. If we are going to say that the New Testament teaches that God has finished with the Jews because they rejected Jesus, then we have to think about how that reconciles with the 'Old' Testament picture.

Also, we do need to address certain issues raised in the New Testament.

Curses on the Jewish Race

In Matthew's gospel, after Pilate had disclaimed responsibility for the blood of Jesus being shed, there is a telling statement *'All the people answered 'let his blood be on us and on our children'.* [1] To quote Stephen the Martyr again in Acts speaking to the Sanhedrin[2] *'They* even killed those who predicted the coming of the Righteous One. And now you have betrayed and murdered him'* [3]

* i.e. their ancestors

35

Such verses have been looked on as a final rejection of the Jews by God as a 'deicidal race'- to put it another way, Christ-killers.

In Matthew 12:22-37 there is a passage where the Pharisees accuse Jesus of casting out demons by 'Beelezebub' (Satan). He goes on to speak about the sin of blasphemy against the Holy Spirit, which is obviously linked to that accusation. The fact that those who made it would not be forgiven (verses 31 & 32) does not mean that God had finished altogether with Israel.

For sure, the judgments of God have continued on the Jews and severe ones at that. The Romans destroyed the Temple in AD 70. During the siege of Jerusalem imposed by the Romans, some Jews resorted to cannibalism. During the years that followed, most of the Jews in Israel were driven out and scattered throughout the whole world. There have been many persecutions of the Jews through the centuries, including the Spanish Inquisition, various massacres, and ultimately the Holocaust.

As far as the persecutions go, the church has sometimes seen fit to add her own judgments to those of the Lord Himself! I give some examples of the horrific things that were done and said to the Jews by the professing church over the centuries later in this chapter. However, God *permitted* them to happen, much as He allowed other nations to successfully attack Israel of old when they were rebellious.

In spite of everything, there remain many promises of restoration and blessing in the 'Old' Testament which seem to point to future times. And, although there have been severe judgments, can we actually take it as far as to say that that God has finally cast them off?

The Jewish Establishment
When we say that the Jews rejected Jesus, to a large extent He was rejected by the Jewish Establishment or leadership,

although there are also indications in the book of Acts that attribute blame to the Jews as a whole such as 2:22-23. Throughout His three years of public ministry, the main problem Jesus had was with members of two of the various Jewish sects of the day- The Pharisees and the Sadducees. They were by and large sceptics. According to Mark 12:37, the common people heard Jesus gladly and there were exceptions among the establishment such as Nicodemus in John.[4]

When it came to the time of the crucifixion, it was the establishment that drove things. Chapters 26 and 27 of Matthew are full of references to 'the chief priests and elders of the people', e.g. *'the chief priests and the whole Sanhedrin were looking for false evidence against Jesus so that they could put him to death'.*[5]

When Jesus came before the reluctant Pilate, *'the chief priests and the elders persuaded the crowd to ask for Barabbas and to have Jesus executed'.*[6]

In the book of Acts, Peter and John are seized and taken before the Sanhedrin for proclaiming the resurrection of Jesus[7] but the number of believers in Jerusalem, who at that time were all Jewish, grew to about 5000[7]. The apostles were arrested by the Sadducees[8] and flogged and the speech leading to Stephen's martyrdom was given to the Sanhedrin[9]. In spite of all this, and more, we read that *'many thousands of Jews have believed and all of them are zealous for the law.'*[10]

Reading the Acts of the Apostles, it is clear that the apostles took a different line when preaching the gospel to Jews on the one hand, and to Greeks on the other. For the Greeks, a good starting point was their poets and philosophers. With the Jews, it was a case of building on the solid foundation of the Torah (Law) and the Prophets, which meant they were ripe for the gospel. It is interesting to speculate whether, had it not been for the intense opposition of Jewish leadership, the vast majority of Jews would have become believers in those early days.

Things haven't changed much. I find that, in our day, once individual Jews show an interest in the gospel, a Rabbi usually pops up to try to put a stop to it. How guilty are individual Jews of rejecting Jesus when their leadership is so determinedly opposed to the gospel?

I even have some sympathy with the problems, on a human level, of the Jewish leaders at the time of Jesus, although clearly they were wrong. As far as we know, Jesus never trained under a particular Rabbi in accordance with the Jewish leadership training system operated then and to the present day. Hence the question the chief priests and elders asked Jesus in Matthew 21:23 *'By what authority are you doing these things....And who gave you this authority?'* This was a massive issue for them. We need to pray for the Jewish leadership of our time, that they will come to faith and lead their people to faith.

We must be cautious anyway of writing the Jews off on the grounds that they, as a nation, rejected and killed the Lord Jesus. In a sense, we *all* killed Jesus because we are *all* sinners.

Having said that, there are two particular New Testament passages we need to look at because some Christians suggest that they prove that God has finished with the Jews.

Matthew 21:43
'Therefore I tell you that the kingdom of God will be taken away from you and given to a people who will produce its fruit'

This is often quoted as a 'proof-text' that God has washed His hands of the Jews as a nation for good. However, what often goes unnoticed is that, if you go back to the start of the conversation in which the above verse is included, you find that Jesus is talking to an elite group- *'The chief priests and the elders of the people'.*[11]

There are a number of interpretations of Matthew 21:43 advanced by various commentators, for example:

38

- The Jewish nation has forfeited its elect status as a nation[12]
- The church will have a Gentile majority[13]
- Jewish leaders will be replaced in leadership by believers who trust in Jesus[14]
- The Jewish generation in the time of Jesus rejected the kingdom, but it will be offered to a later Jewish generation that will accept it[15]

Verse 45 settles the issue of to whom this applies i.e. '...*they knew he was talking about them*'.

Acts 1: 6-8

When Jesus told His disciples to wait in Jerusalem for the coming of the Holy Spirit, they asked him in verse 6 '*Lord, are you at this time going to restore the kingdom to Israel?*' Jesus replied in verse 7 '*It is not for you to know the times or dates the Father has set by his own authority*' and he then reminds them of the immediate business in hand.

Many have read into this passage a denial of a future kingdom for Israel and I am not sure how they manage it! Jesus actually said times and dates had been set but that the disciples didn't need to know the details. If Jesus had wanted to say that there was no question of a future kingdom for Israel, then this would have been the perfect opportunity.

This links with Acts 3:21 '*He (Jesus) must remain in heaven until the time comes for God to restore everything, as he promised long ago through his holy prophets*'. Other passages in the Bible make it clear that the restoration process begins even before Jesus returns.

Unfortunately, this scripture has been taken out of context by the 'Restoration Movement'.[16] They have used it as a major platform for 'Apostles Today', with the highly doubtful idea of the church taking over the world before Jesus comes back to earth.

Another stumbling block for some Christians is the term 'The Seed of Abraham'.

Who are 'The Seed of Abraham?

As I illustrated in chapter 1, Christians sometimes unnecessarily feel that they have to choose between alternative meanings of terms found in the Bible, rather than embrace more than one application.

The 'seed' or 'descendants' or 'offspring' of Abraham are mentioned many times in the Bible, for example in Genesis where God tells Abram that his seed will be like the heavens and stars in number.[17] God said that He would establish His covenant as an everlasting one with Abraham's seed and give the whole land of Canaan as an everlasting possession to them.[18] Abraham had been renamed as a *father of many nations'*. It is important to see the promises to Abraham in Genesis as multi-layered.

Some say, however, that the only valid meaning of the 'seed of Abraham' in New Testament terms is his spiritual descendants, i.e. the church. This is a restrictive interpretation that denies the fact that the term can have different meanings in the New Testament.

In Acts[19], Peter addressing the 'Men of Israel, refers back to Genesis *'In your seed all the nations of the earth shall be blessed'*[20] and in Galatians Paul says *'if you belong to Christ, then you are Abraham's seed, and heirs according to the promise.'*[21] In Romans, Paul counts the promise to Abraham's offspring as *'not only to those who are of the law but also to those who are of the faith of Abraham'*[22], using both physical and spiritual meanings. In Romans 9, he also points out that *'not all who are descended from Israel are Israel'*.[23]

Then, rather than saying it is only the church that has inherited promises, he contrasts the position of the lines of Isaac (Jewish) and Ishmael (Arab) as it is the *former* that are *'children of the promise'*.[24]

In Galatians, Christ Himself is described as the seed of Abraham.[25]

These various passages illustrate the different meanings the term 'Seed of Abraham' has in the New Testament.

Arnold Fruchtenbaum, a Jewish believer and a Bible Teacher, says *'there is no question that Christians are called the spiritual seed of Abraham, but the New Testament never states that they are heirs of the national promises made to the physical descendants and never calls this group* 'Israel'.[26]

The term 'Israel' in the New Testament

This leads on to another area that some Christians are confused about. That is the use of the term 'Israel' in the New Testament. The term 'Israel' is used over 70 times in the New Testament. Only by ignoring the context can it be understood to mean 'the church' rather than the literal Jewish nation.

However, there are a few verses where the meaning of 'Israel' is modified in some way and these are Galatians 6:16, Romans 9:6 and Romans 11:26.

I recommend the reader to go through the references to Israel in the New Testament as listed in Strong's Concordance to verify this. For a fuller explanation see Derek Prince's book 'The Destiny of Israel and the Church' (see Recommended Resources).

We now move on to the issue of 'Replacement Theology', which I mentioned in my Introduction.

The origins of 'Replacement Theology'

The belief that God cast off, or 'unelected', the Jews because they had rejected Jesus and replaced them with the church gradually took hold in the early centuries AD. In AD 70, the

41

Romans destroyed the Second Temple and later expelled the bulk of the Jews from the Land of Israel. The church leaders of the day became convinced that God had therefore demonstrated that Christianity was now the superior faith, entirely displacing Judaism.

This belief persisted over the centuries and, if you go to Strasbourg Cathedral in France, you will see two statues outside which graphically illustrate the assumed displacement of the Synagogue by the Church - See the photographs at the end of this chapter.

This left them with a problem, because there are many passages in the 'Old' Testament that suggest that God's dealings with the Jews are not yet over. Partly due to this, a system of interpretation developed that depended on the use of 'allegory', a term which comes from two Greek words meaning 'to speak other'.

The influence of Greek thought and philosophy was strong in the world in which the church came into being and this meant that the allegorical way of interpretation gained ground. In particular, words like 'Israel', 'Zion', 'Jacob' and 'Jerusalem' no longer had their obvious ordinary meanings. They were said to 'stand for' something else, usually 'the church', and this peculiar approach has persisted in some Christian circles to the present day.

For example, God gathering His children from East, West, North and South and bringing them back to the Land could be taken to mean many people coming into the church.[27] A straightforward, literal reading would be the Jews returning to Israel from all parts of the earth.

This kind of thinking was championed by church leaders such as Origen of Egypt (AD 185-254), Justin Martyr (AD 100-165) and John Chrysostom of Antioch (AD 347-407). The German Protestant theologian Martin Luther (AD 1483-1546) in later life went down this route. Luther wrote *The War Against the*

Jews and, just before his death in 1546, he preached a damning sermon called *'Concerning the Jews and their Lies'*.

The church has been inconsistent over the centuries and sometimes the promises of blessing in the 'Old' Testament have been taken for the church, while the warnings of curses have been left for the Jews! For example, some would say that Isaiah 3 which is headed 'Judgment on Jerusalem' and 'Judah' in the NIV will apply to literal Israel/the Jews. On the other hand, they would say that Isaiah 14:1-2, which talks about 'Jacob' and 'Israel's restoration and blessing can be taken for the church.

Persecutions of the Jews by the 'Church'

The approach I have summarised has fuelled anti-semitism in the church and provided a basis for justifying horrific persecutions of the Jews over the centuries by those claiming to be followers of Christ.[28] Since the fourth century AD, there have been massacres and annihilation, expulsions from lands and countries, withdrawal of certain types of employment and forced baptisms under threat of torture and death. In earlier centuries, Jewish children were kidnapped and Jews were banned from going outdoors at the times of Christian festivals in certain countries.

Jews who converted to Christianity were required to recite carefully prepared statements designed to cut them off from everyone and everything Jewish.

It was not only what was done to them but also was what said. There are many examples in church history books and I will give just two brief ones. John Chrysostom, who was ironically known as 'The Golden-Mouthed', described them as *'worse than wild beasts', 'lustful, rapacious, greedy, perfidious bandits, inveterate murderers, destroyers, men possessed by the devil'*.[29]

Luther posed the question *'What shall we Christians do with this damned, rejected race of Jews?'* and he answered his own question in

43

this way…'*First, their synagogues should be set on fire…Secondly, their homes should likewise be broken down and destroyed… Thirdly, they should be deprived of their prayer books…Fourthly, their rabbis must be forbidden under pain of death to teach any more…Fifthly, passport and travelling privileges should be absolutely forbidden to the Jews….Sixthly, they ought to be stopped from usury….We ought to drive the rascally lazy bones out of our system… Therefore away with them…*[30]

Is it therefore surprising that Germany was the nation that, in a later century, spawned Hitler, the Nazis and the Holocaust?

Symbolism

Excessive use of the idea of symbolism is a factor as well. There is, of course, *some* symbolism and allegory in the Bible but there is usually a justification in the passage for taking words symbolically. Some symbols can be explained by cross-reference to other passages using the same symbols in which the meaning is more obvious.[31] Symbolism, however, can be and often is misused. David L Larsen speaks of '*those who through the centuries have seen the biblical text as a nose of putty to be shaped and formed at will*'[32]

Stephen Sizer's book 'Zion's Christian Soldiers'? [33] contains misrepresentations of Christian Zionist thinking, even allowing for the diversity of thought within Christian Zionism. He bangs a loud drum on the point that the Bible can be taken too literally. In reply, I say I agree but it is equally true that the Bible can be taken *not literally enough!* He speaks, amongst other things, of what he perceives as an 'arbitrary literalism' (page 35). Speaking for myself, my approach to Bible interpretation is anything but arbitrary, but rather it involves a careful contextual consideration of passages. Bishop J C Ryle of the 19th century said '*It is high time for Christians to interpret unfulfilled prophecy by the light of prophecy already fulfilled. The curses on the Jews were brought to pass literally; so also will be the blessings. The scattering was literal; so also will be the gathering. The pulling down of Zion was literal; so also will be the building up. The rejection of Israel was literal; so also will be the restoration'.* [34]

As Josh McDowell says, *'if the literal sense makes good sense, seek no other sense, lest you come up with nonsense!'* [35]

Compromising 'Replacement Theology'?

Whereas some Christians will emphatically say that God has finished with the Jews, others have suggested a compromise. They reject accusations that they endorse 'Replacement Theology' and they agree that the matter of God's covenants is an important one. They agree with the principle that God remains faithful to His people, even when His people don't remain faithful to Him.

God has not cast them off or been unfaithful to them, they say. It's just that the old system where only one nation had a special calling has changed to a new system. In the new system, God's calling is on a people from *all* nations, including believing Jews. One author says its like a child growing up and becoming an adult[36]. There is still a believing holy remnant, as there always has been, so that means God has not cast the Jews off.

This view looks good on the face of it but it breaks down under careful scrutiny. This more subtle approach is still a denial of the uncompleted outworking of God's promises to the race of Israel. It still relies for support on distorting passages of scripture. For example, 'Israel' can mean 'spiritual Israel' or 'the New Israel'. By the 'New Israel', they mean the church, not ethnic Israel. The plain obvious meaning of prophetic passages is avoided and much ink has been used in such futile efforts.

There are isolated verses which, if taken out of context, could look as if they support this view, for example in Galatians[37], *'there is neither Jew nor Greek, slave nor free, male nor female, for you are all one in Christ Jesus'.* But does equality in the Body of Christ

45

between believing Jews and Gentiles mean that there are no practical differences between them? Is their calling identical? The same question can be asked about men and women, and slaves and non-slaves.

The underlying principle is the same regarding males and females and masters and slaves, but here again not all practical differences are done away with. They are of equal status but men and women do not have identical roles. In the early church, masters and slaves worshipped together but still continued in their different positions in society.

At the end of the day, Christians who do not accept that God has an ongoing purpose for the Jews as a nation must answer the question as to why they have been miraculously preserved as a race to the present day, despite all attempts to destroy them. Humanly speaking, they should by now have been either wiped out, or completely merged into other nations with a loss of their distinct identity.

The consequences of Replacement Theology

Adopting Replacement Theology does not necessarily lead anyone to the conclusion that it is the duty of the church to actively persecute the Jews. However, it seems to me from church history that much persecution would have been avoided if the church had not gone down the Replacement Theology route.

In our times, the issue has become much more subtle. Some Christians have a hardness of heart and ingrained prejudice. There is a basic unwillingness to accept that God could still have a use for the Jews *as a people*.

Many of us were brought up hearing and reading jokes and other literature that stereotyped and at times vilified the Jews. I personally had to pray for a real breakthrough in the Holy Spirit before I could love and pray for the Jews, even though I had come to understand the scriptures about them.

Undoubtedly, Replacement Theology adds to a general lack of understanding amongst Christians about events in Israel and Palestine today. Some won't bother to investigate the truth, or otherwise, of the reports churned out by the media. It is so easy to go with the flow and a faulty theology does not help.

If one believes that God discarded his specific plans for the Jews, then there need be no practical response on the lines I set out in my epilogue to this book. No need to pray for Israel, to assist Jews practically or financially, or to make the considerable effort needed to try to understand the issues between Israel and the Church.

Could those who cling to Replacement Theology be vulnerable to falling in line with agendas they should avoid? I am thinking of the Islamic agenda in the Middle East and the agenda of the coming Antichrist, whom many Christians believe will promote a false peace and worldwide 'unity'.

Heresy begets heresy

It seems to me that adopting one major false doctrine can open the gateway to more. As one example, some of those who teach Replacement Theology also teach a 'sister' doctrine known as 'Kingdom Now' or 'Dominion Theology'. This basically says that the church will take over the whole world for Christ before He returns.

Whereas I do believe that there will be a great final harvest of believers, the scriptures clearly show that the earth will not be under the full, evident dominion of Christ's kingdom until a later time period after the return of Jesus. One deception can flow from another and the pride of Replacement Theology can spawn the pride of Dominion Theology.

Conclusion

It is part of the whole mystery of Israel to see that the effect of the rejection of Jesus was to open the way for Gentiles to come to know the Jewish Messiah. Paul says in Romans

11:15…*'their rejection is the reconciliation of the world'* and in 11:25 *'Israel has experienced a hardening in part until the full number of Gentiles has come in.'* I do not believe that God has rejected the Jews because they, or a proportion of them, rejected Jesus. From this standpoint, we go on in the next chapter to look at the restoration of the Jews to the Land of Israel, both from an 'Old' and a New Testament point of view.

The two statues above are 'Ecclesia and Synagoga' as found in the Notre Dame Cathedral in Paris. Such statues are the names given to the symbolic representations in Christian art of the Middle Ages of the victorious Church and defeated Synagogue, symbolising the triumph of Christianity. It became a conventional decoration in many medieval churches. The Church is shown erect and triumphant, while the Synagogue is usually blindfolded and dejected, bearing a broken staff and sometimes decorated with the Tables of the Ten Commandments. They are found in France, England and Germany.

Used under Wikipedia's GNU Free Documentation License

NOTES

1. Matthew 27: 25
2. The Jewish Ruling Council.
3. Acts 7: 52
4. John 3:1-21
5. Matt 26: 59
6. Matt 27:20
7. Acts 4: 1-4
8. Acts 5: 17-18
9. Acts 7
10. Acts 21: 20
11. Matt 21: 23
12. Peake's Commentary on the Bible, Nelson p 791
13. Paraphrased from *The Portable Commentary* by Jamieson, Faussett & Brown, Glasgow William Collins, p 56
14. Paraphrased from David Stern, *Jewish New Testament Commentary*, Jewish New Testament Publications, p 64
15. Paraphrased from *'Israelology'* by Arnold Fruchtenbaum, Ariel Ministries Press, p 822.
16. Part of the Charismatic Movement in the UK beginning in the 1960s and 1970s.
17. Genesis 15:5
18. Genesis 15:18
19. Acts 3:25
20. Genesis 22:18
21. Galatians 3:29

22. Romans 4:16
23. Romans 9:6
24. Romans 9:8
25. Galatians 3:16 & 19
26. From 'Israelology' by Arnold Fruchtenbaum,
    Ariel Ministries Press
27. Isaiah 43:5 & 6
28. See *Our Hands are stained with Blood* by Michael L Brown
    (See Recommended Resources)
29. James Parkes *The Conflict of the Church and the Synagogue*,
    Soncino Press.
30. From *'Concerning the Jews and Their Lies'*, reprinted in
    Talmage, Disputation and Dialogue ps 34-36.
31. Eg compare Revelation 12:1 with Genesis 37: 5-10
32. From *'Israel, The Land and the People'*, H Wayne House,
    Kregel Publications 1998, page 308.
33. Stephen Sizer, Inter-Varsity Press 2007,
34. From *'Are you ready for the end of time?'* p 49,
    Christian Focus Publications, ISBN 1 85792 747 8
35. *'Reasons why we should consider Christianity'* p 32. Scripture
    Press, ISBN 0-946515-52-2. I recommend the section 'Is
    everything in the Bible to be taken literally?' ps 31-33
36. Alan Morrison in an article entitled
    'Abraham our Father, Jerusalem our Mother'.
37. Galatians 3:28

Chapter 4

Exile and Return

In chapter 2, I touched on the subject of exile from and restoration to the Land of Israel. Exile was a consequence of disobedience. There are many warnings of exile and many promises of restoration in the 'Old' Testament and references were given in chapter 2.

In chapter 2, I outlined God's covenants with the Jews. The principle of 'title to the Land of Israel' remaining with the Jews applies even during a period of exile and it goes back to the 'Land Covenant' which I have outlined. Baruch Maoz, an Israeli pastor, has described it as *'the basic covenant which lies at the root of Israel's national existence'*. [1]

In this chapter, I use the terms 'First Return' and 'Second Return'. By the First, I mean the return of the Jews from Babylon only and, by the Second, I mean their return from their worldwide scattering.

Exiles from the Land

In chapter 2, I explained the division between the tribes of Benjamin and Judah ('the Jews') and the other ten tribes ('the Israelites').

During the reign of King Hoshea of Israel, beginning in 732 BC, many of the 'Israelites' were deported to various parts of the Assyrian empire. Some had left the land even before that. There is no timescale given of when they, or their descendants, would return.

Approximately 150 years later, the 'Jews' were exiled to Babylon and God said that in their case there would be a return *exactly* 70 years later. [2] That return *did* begin exactly 70 years later.

Once those exiles returned, they formed the Israel or Hebrew Jews[3], together with those Israelites still in the Land, as opposed to those scattered in other lands. Not all of them returned.

From AD 70 onwards, after the destruction of the Second Temple in Jerusalem, the Romans expelled most of the Jews from Israel. Over the centuries since, Jews have settled in most parts of the world.

Returns to the Land

It is very important to distinguish between the two different returns. Isaiah 11:11 says *'In that day the Lord will reach out his hand a second time to reclaim the remnant that is left of his people from Assyria, from Lower Egypt, from Upper Egypt, from Cush, from Elam, from Babylonia, from Hamath, and from the islands of the sea'.*

The first time was the return from Babylon, only from North and South. The late Bible teacher, Derek Prince, identifies the above areas with modern equivalents in brackets as: Assyria (mainly Iraq), Lower and Upper Egypt (Egypt), Cush (probably Ethiopia), Elam (Iran), Babylonia (mainly Iraq), Hamath (Syria) and 'the islands of the sea' (arguably all modern continents).[4] Isaiah 43:5-6 speaks of a return from north, south, east and west, and *'from afar'* and *'from the ends of the earth'*.

Clearly the return from Babylon was not permanent but, by contrast, the scriptures indicate that the worldwide return is. Amos 9:14 says *'I will bring back my exiled people Israel…'* and 9:15 says *'I will plant Israel in their own land, never again to be uprooted from the land I have given them…'*

Ezekiel 37:25 says *'They will live in the land I gave to my servant Jacob, the land where your fathers lived. They and their children and their children's children will live there forever…'*

(The Hebrew word *'olam'* translated here as 'forever' can mean 'eternal' or 'age-lasting', i.e. for a very, very long time).

In Ezekiel 37:22, God promises to reunite the twelve tribes in the Land, healing the old division.

We are told in the Bible how long it would be before the return from Babylon, but not how long it would be before the return from the worldwide scattering.

The First Return was a literal event. Should we not adopt a consistent approach and expect the Second Return to be likewise, rather than just looking for a 'spiritual' meaning in the prophetic passages?

Is the Second Return in unbelief?

This issue is something of a 'hot potato'. In chapter 6 on Britain and Israel, I comment on British Christians of the seventeenth to nineteenth centuries who looked for a return of the Jews to the Land. They were divided on the question as to whether or not a mass conversion of Jews to Christ had to come *before* a return.

Many Christians have a problem with believing that what we are seeing *is* God's doing because the majority of the Jews have not yet come to faith in Jesus. Many of them are not religious at all. Furthermore, the media with its often negative and biased portrayal of Israel heavily influences many Christians (see chapter 5).

There are even Orthodox Jewish sects, both in Israel and elsewhere, who do not believe modern-day Israel is from God. They point to the ungodliness in Israel, e.g. the high abortion rate and secularism, and they believe that only the Messiah himself personally can bring the Jews back.

I can understand these reservations and, let's face it, in some ways modern Israel at the moment is no more holy than modern Britain! However, God is God and he can do things any way He chooses. The Bible passages dealing with the Second Return are numerous and, having analysed them all, it seems to me that the majority of them suggest that the return *precedes* spiritual revival. Two important passages are Ezekiel 36 and Jeremiah 32, to which I refer later in this chapter.

Those passages suggest that God specifically wants to deal with them *in the Land*, which means of course that they have to get there first. And, what's more, stay alive there, which is an important point when it comes to thinking about what Israel does in terms of security measures.

One anti-Zionist Jew maintains that *'Zionism is a philosophy originated by non believers, by Jews long since estranged from their faith'*. [5] It is true that the leading Zionist Theodor Herzl, who foresaw the modern Jewish State 50 years before its founding, and some early other Zionists, were not God-fearing. However, the reviver of the Hebrew language, Eliezer Ben-Yehuda, in 1918 wrote *'In those days it was as if the heavens had suddenly opened, and a clear incandescent light flashed before my eyes and a mighty inner voice sounded in my ears 'the resurrection of Israel on its ancestral soil'...* [6]

In Nehemiah 1:8-9, Nehemiah reminds the Lord of his words to Moses *'...if you are unfaithful, I will scatter you among the nations, but if you return to me and obey my commands, then even if your exiled people are at the farthest horizon, I will gather them to the place I have chosen as a dwelling place for my Name.'*

And yet, the Lord brought them back from Babylon as they were anyway. In the same way, it seems to me that He is bringing them back from all over the world as they are, but not yet as He wants them to be. Why? Simply because the Lord's time has come. Psalm 102:13 says *'you will arise and have compassion on Zion, for it is time to show favour to her; the appointed time has come...'*

Is there not a parallel here with how God deals with individual Christians? God brings us back to His purposes for our lives in spite of our disobedience.

Geographical and Spiritual Restoration

Christian Zionists are sometimes charged with striving to fit contemporary events into the biblical prophecies. Well, I would counter with pointing out that some things obviously fit the prophecies! However, to be as helpful as possible to the critics I am using some material from a book written in 1944 and updated in 1946, shortly *before* the modern State of Israel was established. John Wilkinson, Founder of the Mildmay Mission to the Jews, writes a chapter in his book *'God's Plan For the Jew'* on 'Restoration'.

He begins as follows *'Will the elect nation of Israel ever return to the land of their fathers? Many Christians say, No; many other Christians say, Yes. Those who deny the future restoration of the nation contend that all the prophecies relating to restoration were fulfilled on the return from Babylonish captivity, or that they are to be spiritualised and referred to the Church.'* [7]

Wilkinson saw that if the worldwide scattering of national Israel was literal, then so must there be a literal regathering of national Israel. He also said *'The scriptures further teach that the Jews are to be restored in unbelief'.* [8]

He relies mainly for this on chapters 36 and 37 of Ezekiel, e.g. 36:24-28- *'For I will take you out of the nations; I will gather you from all the countries and bring you back into your own land. I will sprinkle clean water on you, and you will be clean; I will cleanse you from all your impurities and from all your idols.'*

He also quotes Jeremiah 32, e.g. vs 37- *'I will surely gather them from all the lands where I banish them in my furious anger and great wrath; I will bring them back to this place and let them live in safety. They will be my people, and I will be their God. I will give them singleness of heart and action, so that they will always fear me…I will make an everlasting covenant with them…I will inspire them to fear me, so that they will never turn away from me. I… will assuredly plant them in this land with all my heart and soul.'*

The well-known commentator Matthew Henry, when dealing with Ezekiel 37:25-26, says …*'They shall dwell in the land of Israel. They shall have it by covenant; they shall come in again upon their old title, by virtue of the grant made unto Jacob, God's servant…They are beloved for their fathers' sakes. They shall dwell therein for all time…'* [9]

Many Bible passages may look to a casual reader as if they describe events that are simultaneous, but there is no reason to assume that. God is not in a hurry and there can be a significant time gap between stages of His plan. I suspect that there is a touch of Christian self-righteousness underlying the idea that the Jews cannot be restored to the land in unbelief. Perhaps some feel that, after nearly 2000 years, the Jews don't deserve any favours and God can do without them anyway.

Natural factors

There are many evidences of God's hand in natural ways on the restored nation of Israel, eg many scientific and medical breakthroughs by Jews. There are of course negative factors as we look at the Jews, but *surely* we can see supernatural factors at work. Take, for example, their victories in various wars against overwhelming odds and their significant irrigation and reclamation projects in desert areas.

The revival of the ancient Hebrew language, which began in the nineteenth century but has come into its own since 1948 in Israel, is remarkable and unprecedented. Ancient languages that have become disused do not usually become written and spoken again.

Ezekiel's Vision of The Valley of Dry Bones

Wilkinson says that Ezekiel's vision in chapter 37 *'graphically sets forth the restoration of the nation, followed by national conversion; then under the figure of the union of two sticks, Judah and Israel, is set forth the union of the twelve tribes, forming "one nation in the land", with "one king" over them all; and a "covenant of peace" made with them…Then shall the knowledge of Israel's restoration and sanctification be extended to the Gentile nations'*[10]

I recommend a study of chapters 36 and 37 of Ezekiel. His vision of the 'Valley of Dry Bones' in chapter 37 clearly suggests a stage-by-stage restoration of Israel. However, some 'de-programming' may be necessary as many of us have heard sermons where those verses have been taken as predicting revival for the church. That could be appropriate as an *extension* of the meaning, but it is not the *primary literal* meaning.

In chapter 36, God tells us in verses 20 to 24 that *His* holy name has been profaned due to the worldwide scattering and that He intends to put that to rights by taking them back to their own land. Verses 25 to 29 describe a spiritual cleansing and revival and then the verses that follow switch back and forth from spiritual cleansing to the blossoming of the actual land. The impression given is that, while the Land *itself* may be fruitful to some extent *before* the spiritual cleansing, it will be much more so *during and after.*

Note also in verses 12 and 13 of chapter 37, God speaks of opening the *graves* of his people. This suggests the people of Israel being at a very low ebb indeed and seems consistent with their condition after the Holocaust.

In a similar way, chapters 12 to 14 of Zechariah paint a vivid picture of God's dealings with His re-gathered people in the Land of Israel. Note in particular 13:1 '*On that day a fountain will be opened to the house of David and the inhabitants of Jerusalem, to cleanse them from sin and impurity*'. This surely implies that the Jews are already *in Israel* before this remarkable work of God takes place. It is unlikely that God would allow a time of rigorous judgment to fall on them if they were already an obedient, believing nation. Rather, many of them will come to faith in the Land after a time of purging.

Turning to contemporary issues in Israel, both the military and the spiritual battle for Israel are huge. Just a few of the issues are drug addiction, witchcraft and New Age influence and abortion. This is why many groups have developed which meet to pray for Israel.[11]

The New Testament and the Land of Israel

A common objection to belief in a Second Return is the idea that the right of the Jews to the Land of Israel is not confirmed in the New Testament.

Firstly, even if that were true, which it is not, it flies in the face of the Christian claim that we accept the *whole Bible*. Jesus, in Matthew 5: 17 & 18 says *'Do not think I have come to abolish the Law or the Prophets; I have not come to abolish them but to fulfil them. I tell you the truth, until heaven and earth disappear, not the smallest letter, not the least stroke of a pen, will by any means disappear from the Law until everything is accomplished.'*

Included in 'the Law and the Prophets' is much about the right of the Jews to the Land of Israel. We may think that we can get round this by saying that Christ has 'fulfilled' all the promises in the Law and the Prophets, bringing the issue of the land to a close. However, the Greek word often translated 'fulfil' can have various meanings, including 'fill', 'fill up', 'fill out', or 'make full'.

Have heaven and earth disappeared yet? It doesn't look that way to me!

Turning to the New Testament, let us ask the question 'does there *need* to be a repetition or affirmation of 'Old' Testament teaching about the Land? It is fully covered in the 'Old' Testament. Wouldn't it be more appropriate to ask 'do we find a *denial* on the subject in the New Testament'?

Of course we don't! James Walker, in 'Israel-Covenant and Land', argues… *'the presence of Israel in the land is assumed right through the New Testament, and indeed, most of the New Testament books were written prior to the destruction of Jerusalem in 70 AD…*[12]

Of course, the New Testament does not deny that the Jews could still be expelled again from the land for disobedience, as set out in the 'Old' Testament. In chapter 3, we saw that there was a rejection of Jesus as Messiah by the Jewish establishment. This led eventually to a separation between the main Jewish community and the Messianic Jews (believers in

Jesus). The Romans destroyed the Second Temple in AD 70 and, by the middle of the next century, most Jews had left the Land.

Romans 15:8 says ... *'Christ has become a servant of the Jews on behalf of God's truth, to confirm the promises made to the patriarchs...'* Some may dismiss this with a wave of the hand on the grounds that all the promises are 'fulfilled' in the death and resurrection of Jesus. Is this another example of the 'Either/Or Mentality' of the Church which I talk about in chapter 1? Do we have to choose between *spiritual* or *physical* fulfilment, or can it be both?

Tony Higton, a former Rector of Christchurch, Jerusalem, wrote in 'Shalom', the magazine of the Church's Ministry Among Jewish People, *'I agree wholeheartedly with those who say that eschatology (the doctrine of the End Times) is about Jesus and the promises fulfilled in him...but that should not lead us to neglect or deny the other teaching of scripture about the end times and one aspect is the return to Israel. I find it unbelievable that some Christians regard the parallel between this event and biblical prophecy to be merely coincidental. That beggars belief...'*

For further study on this aspect, I recommend a booklet by Chuck Cohen called 'Grounded-The Promised Land in the New Testament'. Available from Christian Friends of Israel (see Recommended Resources) or the author of this book-email address: theheartofthematter@hotmail.co.uk

Does Israel have all the Land yet?

In Genesis 15:18, God says to Abraham *'to your descendants I will give this land, from the river of Egypt to the great river, the Euphrates'...* One writer estimates that the amount of land involved in that description would be roughly two and a half times the size of the British Isles. In contrast, the present size of Israel is about the size of Wales only. Are there enough Jews in the world to fill all that space? Only the Lord knows, but they are probably more numerous than we think as some have no knowledge of their Jewish identity.

Some point to 1 Kings 4:21 as a complete fulfilment of Genesis 15:18...*'and Solomon ruled over all the kingdoms from the River to the land of the Philistines, as far as the border of Egypt. These countries brought tribute and were Solomon's subjects all his life'.* The NIV footnote states that 'the River' is the Euphrates. However, there is no suggestion here that all those areas were actually occupied or possessed by the Israelites, but rather that much of the land was only *under tribute* to Solomon.

There is no evidence anywhere in the Bible that the Jews ever occupied the entirety of the Promised Land and it remains to be seen how and when God will bring about the ultimate fulfilment of His covenant promise. It could be that it will partly be after the time when 'all Israel shall be saved' (Romans 11:26), which I deal with in chapter 7.

All this talk of a land may seem very unspiritual to Christian eyes, but we need to remember that the most important thing about the Land of Israel is what God intends to do there. It has a strong connection with the Second Coming of Jesus and with the whole world (see chapter 7).

Israel is God's Land

It would be good to end this chapter by pointing out some important things. The next chapter moves to the controversial Israel/Palestine debate. It is vital to see that, at the end of the day, Israel is *God's land*.

In Deuteronomy 11:12, we read *'it is a land the LORD your God cares for; the eyes of the LORD your God are continually on it from the beginning of the year to its end'*.

In Joel 3:1-2, God says *'...when I restore the fortunes of Judah and Jerusalem, I will gather all nations and bring them down to the Valley of Jehoshaphat. There I will enter into judgment against them concerning my inheritance, my people Israel, for they scattered my people among the nations and divided up my land...'*

Finally, the restoration of Israel is not for Israel's sake- but ultimately *for God's holy name's sake* (see Ezekiel 36:20-23)- see chapter 7. Having set out introductory material from the scriptures, I turn in the next chapter to some of the more historical and contemporary issues about Israel.

NOTES

1. Paper entitled *Israel, People, Land, State and Torah* presented at the Third International Consultation on Jewish Evangelism in 1986 and available from Mishkan magazine on the Internet.
2. Jeremiah 25:11-12 & 29:10 & Daniel 9:2.
3. See Acts 6:1.
4. Slightly paraphrased from page 57 of *The Last Word on The Middle East* (Zondervan Corporation, Grand Rapids, Michigan 1982)
5. www.nkusa.org/activities/speeches/nyc041202.cfm
6. www.benyehuda.us/Default.htm
7. John Wilkinson, *God's Plan For The Jew*, p 47, The Paternoster Press 1946, no ISBN
8. Same, p 52.
9. Matthew Henry's *Commentary on the Whole Bible*, Marshall, Morgan & Scott, p 1073
10. John Wilkinson, *God's Plan For The Jew*, p 52
11. There are many groups meeting throughout the UK to pray for Israel and the surrounding nations. Prayer For Israel is probably the leading organisation in this field. See the list of Recommended Resources for their details and those of other Israel-related Christian organisations.
12. *Israel, Covenant and Land*, James B Walker, Handsel Press, ISBN 0 905312 55 4, p 7

Chapter 5

Israel and Palestine

Introduction

The previous chapter outlined some of the issues about 'Exile and Return'. This points to the fact that the modern State of Israel is an ongoing fulfilment of relevant biblical prophecy, even if it doesn't look much like it at times to the 21st century Christian.

Having a scriptural foundation is essential, otherwise what basis do Christians have to assess the historical and media accounts that we come across? We need to ask questions about the possible underlying agenda of the writer or journalist. Are they hostile to parts or even all of the scriptures and therefore to God's agenda? Again, perhaps it is not hostility but a lack of understanding.

Unfortunately, having a scriptural foundation will not immediately answer every question we want an answer to. When it comes to things 'on the ground' concerning Israel, some things take time to weigh up. I sympathise with the struggles some Christians have.

Some Christians say that the modern State of Israel, created in 1948, is not a fulfilment of Bible Prophecy. If that is the case, then it is interesting to ponder why Satan stirred up Hitler to try to liquidate the Jews in the 1940s. It reminds me of the way that Satan stirred up Herod to kill all the baby boys of a similar age to Jesus in an attempt to thwart God's imminent purposes. The Jews, a race of people small in numbers, have survived to the present day despite all attempts to destroy them. Many of them have returned to the land of their ancestors, have revived an ancient language, engaged in significant forms of industry and defended themselves against overwhelming odds.

We must surely believe that this is highly significant and that God is at work in a miraculous way, even if the human aspects of the situation perplex us.

We now go on to take a brief look at some of the historical and contemporary issues regarding the Land of Israel and the adjacent territories. Many books, articles and reports refer to the territories taken by Israel in the 1967 War as 'Occupied Territories' but, in my opinion, it would be more accurate to call them 'Disputed Territories'.

Vast amounts of material have been written on this subject. Accounts vary from those that merely differ on points of detail to radically diverging versions of events with little, if any, common ground. Steve Maltz, a British Jew who believes in Jesus, has said *'Millions of words have been written and spoken about it.....Jews and Zionists will tell you one thing and Arabs and Arabists will tell you the opposite!'*[1]

The media on the whole, with some notable exceptions, tends to demonise Israel as an aggressive, occupying power bent on genocide and ethnic cleansing. The Palestinians are the underdogs, oppressed by the mighty Jews, despite the fact that the Arab states surrounding Israel have a combined land mass 660 times greater than that of Israel.[2] One example of bias has been the media portrayal of the Gaza Flotilla incident of May 2010. A small number of partly-armed Muslim Radicals hijacked an aid expedition amongst hundreds of innocent people. The aim, which succeeded, was to make it look as if the Israelis attacked their ship and killed men without any provocation.

Sadly, some Christians seem to sympathise with the media bias. But have they done their homework? For sure, Israel has built up a very strong military, but what will happen to Israel and her citizens if they lose just one war?

There is a joke about an Israeli Prime Minister who once said to a group of journalists that he was on the following morning due to go on a tour of friendly countries. One of the group piped up and asked him 'Prime Minister - then what are you going to do tomorrow afternoon?'

On the other hand, some Christian Zionists have taken a 'rosy-tinted spectacles' view about Israel and gloss over some of the earthy reality of the last 60 years. This has understandably put other Christians off. Bear in mind though that, as Christian Zionists tend to defend Israel when most of the world and church condemn, it is easy for them to fall into the trap of being overly defensive.

I am impressed with the wise advice of a Jewish Christian called Richard Wolff, who says:

> 'For a Christian, it is essential to retain a genuine Christian perspective. In the heat of rhetoric and passionate emotion this is not easy. At this point it is hardly necessary to point out that both Israel and the Arab nations are at fault. One-sided condemnations or endorsements are not helpful. It is not necessary for the Christian to endorse every act of the Israeli government simply because the nation exists in harmony with God's sovereign purpose.

> Nor is it wise to identify with the Arab refugees to the point of condemning every Israeli action, violently siding with the Arabs. It is essential to retain a genuinely independent, Christian point of view not unduly influenced by presumed knowledge of God's secret purposes, nationalistic feelings (pro-USA, pro-UK, etc), nor emotionally unbalanced by an overemphasis on the plight and misery of refugees. All these factors must become part of the Christian consideration but, in isolation, none of them can be the determining factor'. [3]

While having due regard for what Richard Wolff says, bear in mind that God does say in Genesis 17:20-21 referring to Abraham's sons. *'And as for Ishmael, I have heard you: I will surely bless him; I will make him fruitful and will greatly increase his numbers. He will be the father of twelve rulers*, and I will make him into a great nation. But my covenant is with Isaac...'* The 'covenant' includes the land, mentioned in the same chapter and elsewhere.

(*See Genesis 25:12-18. Both there and in later history, God has fulfilled his promises to the line of Ishmael, with oil wealth and lands and so on. He is also honouring His promises to the line of Isaac with the land of Israel.)

Neither the issue of Jewish nor the issue of Arab descent are wholly straightforward. However, as a rough guide, one can say that the Arabs come from Ishmael and the Jews from Isaac. Now let's unpack some of the issues about which arguments rage.

The origins of the name 'Palestine'

Many Bible maps and commentaries refer to *'Palestine in the time of Christ'* giving rise to the false impression that this is a term which was in use at that time. The term 'Palestine' or 'Palestina' does appear in the King James Version[4], but the correct translation is 'Philistia'- The territory of the Philistines. This error has been corrected in later Bible versions. In the New Testament, the term *'Israel'* is used, even in the KJV.[5]

Many Jews were expelled from the Land (referred to in Matthew 2:20 as *'the Land of Israel')* in the first and second centuries AD. The Romans then renamed it *'Syria Palestina'* in an attempt to erase all Jewish connection with it. Over the centuries, however, the name was rarely used until relatively recent times when it has become a standard term of reference used by writers of all persuasions. The major push for the use of the name has come since the creation in the 1960s of the

Palestine Liberation Organisation, which came with the Palestine National Covenant avowing the destruction of Israel.

A powerful propaganda machine was created. With the use of the name 'Palestine' in our day has come the popular concept of a Palestinian people and nation. These have supposedly existed for countless generations and have been dispossessed by the invading Zionist Jews.

Randall Price, in *Fast Facts on the Middle East Conflict* p 62 (See Recommended Resources), quotes Roger Carasso who says *'The Arabs learned their disinformation tactic from the Nazis: If you repeat the lie long enough, and loud enough, people will actually believe you. As a result, most people now believe there is something called the 'Palestinian' people, a total fabrication, complete with a phony history and a phony culture'.*

There are many examples of such disinformation and many are listed and refuted in detail in the book by Mitchell Bard recommended at the end of this chapter. For example, *'The Jews have no claim to the land they call Israel'*, *'Palestine was always an Arab country'*, *'The Zionists made no effort to compromise with the Arabs'* and *'The British allowed Jews to flood Palestine while Arab immigration was tightly controlled'* (all from p 24 of his book). Also, *'The Temple Mount has always been a Muslim holy place and Judaism has no connection to the site'* (p 277).

Despite the foregoing, to aid understanding, I will use the terms 'Palestine' and 'Palestinians' in the rest of this chapter in the way they are commonly understood.

The refugee issues
Despite varying accounts and emphases, it is clear that in the wake of the establishment of Israel in 1948 both an Arab and a Jewish refugee problem came about.

The Arab refugee problem
Some Arabs in Palestine in 1948 were removed from their homes by Israeli troops or left them because of fear of the

Israeli army. However, around 30,000 wealthy Palestinians had left for neighbouring Arab countries in 1947 in anticipation of war, followed by other Arabs hoping to find work with them.

In 1948, thousands more Arabs left Palestine because of warnings from various Arab leaders to evacuate, on a temporary basis. This was before the Arab invasion of Israel in 1948 which became known as the War of Independence. The evidence for this departure is hotly disputed but Randall Price in *Fast Facts on the Middle East Conflict* cites Arab sources of the time. Those sources make it clear that there was an element of threatening and coercion on the part of Arab leaders.

We must not forget that it is normal and natural in *any and every* war that some people will flee the area if they can. The 'Six Day War' of 1967 created a further wave of Arab refugees.

Estimates of the number of Arab refugees that resulted immediately from the establishment of modern Israel vary widely from around 470,000 to 1,000,000. There appears to be no indisputable official source of information on this.

The population today of Israel is around 7 million. Of these, around 5.6 million are Jews and around 1.4 million are Arabs. Those Arabs are known as 'Israeli Arabs' in contrast to 'Palestinian Arabs' who live in the territories next to Israel. Israeli Arabs are Israeli citizens, although there is debate as to whether they have full rights.

Arab refugee camps
Israel is surrounded by Arab nations and, as stated in the introduction in this chapter, they total a land mass over 600 times that of Israel (see the map at the end of this chapter). Also, some of those nations are rich. There are two astonishing facts. Firstly, that the refugees were not absorbed successfully into those various Arab nations after 1948. Secondly, after 60 years, over a million of the original refugees and their descendants still live as refugees.

A popular notion is that it is the fault, if not the deliberate policy, of Israel that this tragic situation has been unresolved for so long. However, the evidence suggests that the Arab refugees have been used as pawns in a wider struggle, for propaganda purposes and for fuelling world opinion against Israel.

Historian Andrew Roberts, with reference to the Arab League, says '*For many of its governments, which are rich enough to have solved the Palestinian refugee problem decades ago, it is useful to have Israel as a scapegoat to divert attention from the tyranny and corruption of its regimes. The tragic truth is that it suits Arab states to have Palestinians endure permanent refugee status*' [6]

The refugee camps have become a breeding ground for Islamic extremism and 'martyr culture'. Islamic considerations are very important when it comes to understanding the Israeli situation, but a final word first on the subject of refugees.

The Jewish refugee problem

Until 1948, Jews had lived in most Arab Muslim countries in the Middle East. However, in 1948, Jews were expelled from Iraq, Egypt, Libya, Syria, Lebanon, Yemen, Tunisia, Morocco and Algeria. Property was confiscated worth huge amounts of money. It is estimated that around 820,000 Jews became refugees and around 590,000 of them were somehow absorbed into Israel, being a major achievement for the fledgling nation.

Therefore, the Jewish refugee problem was solved but the Arab one remains. It should also be noted that some Arabs came into Israel after 1948 because they saw better economic prospects for their lives.

Israel was responsible for the expulsion of a proportion of the pre-1948 population of Palestine. However, this can be put into perspective by this quote from a 1968 article in the LA Times by Eric Hoffer, a Gentile...'The Jews are a peculiar

69

people; things permitted to other nations are forbidden the Jews. Other nations drive out thousands, even millions of people, and there is no refugee problem. Russia did it. Poland and Czechoslovakia did it. Turkey threw out a million Greeks and Algeria a million Frenchmen…but in the case of Israel, displaced Arabs have become eternal refugees. Everyone insists Israel must take back every single Arab…'

Has the USA ever given the North American Indians a state? Over two million people have in recent years been driven from their homes in the Sudan - is the whole world demanding their right of return?

Islamic considerations
It is easy to underestimate the impact of radical Islam on the relationship between Israel and the surrounding peoples. In the following section, I use the term *'Islamist'* rather than *'Muslim'* in some instances. This is to make an essential distinction between radical and moderate Muslims.

'Taqiyya'
This Arabic word means 'dissimulation' or 'deception'. The concept originated in early Islam as a defence mechanism for persecuted Muslims who were, in effect, licensed to lie to avoid serious trouble. As time went on, this also became an offensive weapon connected with the expansion of Islam. It is practised in the Israel/Palestine conflict, as well as in countries such as the UK where it looks as if there is a long-term strategy to dominate. One example is the manipulation of photographs, sometimes apparently with the co-operation of anti-Israel reporters, which are then transmitted round the world.

Another example is the Hamas tactic of their leaders deliberately hiding in areas and buildings which also contain innocent civilians, so that Israel can then be accused of targeting civilians.

'Disproportionate' responses by Israel?

There is a tendency for the world to 'gang up' on Israel at times and condemn their actions of self-defence as 'disproportionate'. This happened in the war with Hezbollah (in Lebanon) in 2006 and it happened with regard to the attack on Hamas (in Gaza) in late 2008 and early 2009.

I am at a loss to know how people feel they are in a position to make such a snap judgment and I wonder what *they* would do if they had to deal with such terribly difficult situations. A factor is that there has been a much greater number of Palestinian as opposed to Israeli casualties in conflicts such as the ones just mentioned.

This is the inevitable result of fighting militias that are relatively less prepared and trained than the Israeli Defence Forces are. Combined with this is the deliberate policy of Palestinian terrorist groups of using their own civilians as shields. It should be borne in mind that Gaza is one of the most densely populated places on Earth. The aim is to turn world opinion more and more against Israel by making it look as if they deliberately target civilians.

The anti-Israel clamour of world opinion seems to get harsher and more strident with each successive clash between Israel and her enemies. It is not difficult to see how this could, one day, lead to the situation described by Zechariah in chapters 12 to 14, that is when all nations gather against Jerusalem.

The illogical nature of anti-semitism is clearly illustrated by the massive international witch-hunt which has been going on following on from Operation Cast Lead, the Israeli invasion of Gaza around the turn of 2009. This apparently seeks to bring Israeli leaders to justice for alleged 'war crimes'. Hamas, however, who are not averse to murdering fellow Muslims if it

71

suits their purposes, seem relatively undisturbed. If anything is disproportionate, this is!

Israel does not seem to have such quick, decisive victories as in some of the earlier wars (see Chronology of Key Events since 1896). Perhaps this is because, as a nation, Israel has strayed further from God.

For a more detailed explanation of the major issues faced by Israel in conflicts, see Appendix 3.

Claiming territory for 'Allah'

Once territory has been taken for Islam, it is intended that it remain eternally Islamic. Islamists therefore can never be content while, for example Spain, which was once Islamic, remains 'Christian'. In the same way, the area now known as 'Israel' was for centuries under Islamic rule and simply *cannot* be allowed to stay that way.

The prominent British Muslim Yusuf Islam (formerly Cat Stevens) has said *'Palestine is Islamic ground. One day the flag of Islam will be flying all over the world.'*[7]

According to the September issue of Israel Today magazine (p18), a handbook for elementary school teachers in Jordan, says…*'If Jews own even one centimetre of Arab land, jihad becomes the inevitable duty of every Muslim.'*

Those who are persuaded that there should be a Palestinian State alongside Israel fail to realise that it could be an Islamic Republic which would militate against Israel. It could also be the 'final nail in the coffin' of the already beleaguered Palestinian Christians. Would a Palestinian State satisfy the Palestinians? Might it not mean more opportunity to fire missiles at Israel in the same way as been the case with Gaza since the Israelis withdrew in 2005? Is the issue really Israel's *land* or Israel's *existence*?

The late former Israeli Prime Minister, Yitzhak Rabin, said *'a Palestinian State will rise upon the ruins of the State of Israel'*. To put

72

it another way, in the June 2009 Watchmen's Prayer Letter (Christian Friends of Israel), Frank and Karen Selch write *'If the PA (*Palestinian Authority*) receives all its demands, what is left of Israel will be a nation with indefensible borders surrounded by hostile neighbours that have indoctrinated successive generations of their children with hatred and the lies that the Jews are a cancer on the human race and need to be exterminated!'*

All overtures promising long term peace in exchange for the giving up of land covenanted by God to the Jews are subject to both *taqiyya* and to Islamist ideas about 'truces' or 'ceasefires', which I will explain, using an Arabic term.

'Hudna'

A *hudna*, often translated as 'cease-fire', is a truce for a specified period. From the point of view of the Islamists, they have no intention of sticking to the bargain. They are regrouping, in other words waiting until they are in a stronger position to take ground. Historically, Mohammed made a ten year *hudna* with the Quraysh tribe who ruled Mecca in the seventh century. Two years into the *hudna,* he broke it on a pretext and conquered Mecca.

Both the late Yasser Arafat in his day, with the Oslo Accords, and Hamas in recent times, have demonstrated clearly how these principles operate. A six month ceasefire was agreed in June 2008 with Hamas, but broken by an early resumption of rocket attacks on Israel. This resulted regrettably, but inevitably, in a military response from Israel in December 2008.

There is an ongoing struggle between Islamists and nations that are not yet Islamic Republics known as 'Jihad'. This can be military, ideological, or both. The danger of military Jihad is an ever-present one for Israel.

In saying all this, I am not ignorant of the fact that many Muslims would see Israel as a secular, Westernised state bringing a corrupting influence into their area of the world. If we add to this the ever-lingering memory of the medieval Crusades and a sense of oppression by British Colonialism, then we can avoid judging them too harshly.

The condition of Palestine in the nineteenth century

Part of the campaign by modern-day 'Palestinians' for their perceived rights revolves around a dubious claim that they and their ancestors have lived in and owned land in Palestine for hundreds, if not thousands, of years. A more extreme Palestinian revision of history is that there never was a Jewish presence in the land, there were no temples in Jerusalem, and Kings David and Solomon never existed.

I am obviously not saying there were no Arabs in the land before 1948 but consider the following statements made by those who travelled to Palestine in the nineteenth century:

'Of all the lands there are for dismal scenery, I think Palestine must be the prince...It is a hopeless, dreary, heart-broken land...Palestine sits in sackcloth and ashes. Over it broods the spell of a curse that has withered its fields and fettered its energies...' [8] (see Deuteronomy 29:23)

'No national union and no national spirit has prevailed there. The motley impoverished tribes which have occupied it have held it as mere tenants at will, temporary landowners, evidently waiting for those entitled to the permanent possession of the soil'... [9]

Why Palestine for the Jews?

First and foremost, the answer lies in the scriptures about God's covenants (see chapter 2). However, in human terms, the following quote is interesting and is taken from conversations between a Jew, Chaim Weizmann, (see also chapter 6) and a British politician.

In the years before the Balfour Declaration (see chapter 6), a member of the House of Lords asked Chaim Weizmann *'Why do you Jews insist on Palestine when there are so many undeveloped*

74

countries you could settle in more conveniently?'. Weizmann replied *'That is like my asking you why you drove twenty miles to visit your mother last Sunday when there are so many old ladies living on your street'*. [10]

Obviously I am convinced that the Jews have a covenant right to the Land of Israel. However, I have already conceded that their behaviour is not all it should be. Here are some examples of wrong behaviour from both sides.

Jewish and Arab incidents
I give selected examples below. All places mentioned are in Israel.

Jewish
History records an episode involving the Arabs who at one time lived in a village called Biram (or Berram). The Israeli army came and told the villagers that, for their own safety, they were being temporarily moved to another nearby village, but they would soon be allowed back to Biram. For reasons which do not appear clear to me, the villagers were never allowed to return to their homes, although they were given housing elsewhere. Even more recent attempts to address this situation appear to have failed.

In 1948, two Jewish groups called *Irgun* and the *Stern Gang* attacked an Arab village called Deir Yassin, close to Jerusalem. As with most incidents in the history of modern Israel, the details are much disputed. Estimates in reports of Arabs killed vary between 100 and 250. Jewish sources insist that warnings were given to the inhabitants to leave before the action was taken. The Jews were accused of deliberately firing on women but, in reply, said that some of the Arab men had disguised themselves as women.

The reason given for the attack was that the village had been used by Arab snipers who fired on convoys of vehicles carrying essential supplies to Jerusalem on the only available road.

Other sources, however, say the attack was to inspire panic in the Arabs and a possibly a revenge attack for the destruction of two Jewish settlements.

Some Arab sources described it as a bloodbath, accusing the perpetrators of murdering old people and children and ripping open pregnant women. There is a lack of proof of those allegations in interviews with survivors of the attack. An organisation called the Jewish Agency reacted with horror and disgust at the attack, as did other Jewish officials.

In 1949, Irgun blew up a wing of the King David Hotel in Jerusalem. Ninety-one people were killed, some of whom were British. The Jews were very frustrated with the British administration. The British had confiscated large numbers of documents about the operations of Irgun. Some say that warnings were issued before this attack.

Also there have been random attacks on Arabs carried out on occasions by individual Jews. There was an attack on the Muslim section of the Cave of Patriarchs in Hebron in 1994 by a Jewish settler named Baruch Goldstein. Between 30 and 50 Muslims were shot dead and many were injured. The late Yitzhak Rabin, who at the time was the Israeli Prime Minister, in a telephone conversation with the late Yasser Arafat, described the attack as 'a loathsome, criminal act of murder'. A later enquiry found Goldstein guilty. However, some 'Right Wing' Jewish extremists have venerated Goldstein's memory. As with any topic, the Internet is replete with articles on the subject, some of which exonerate Goldstein from blame as having been 'set up' by the Israeli Security Services.

Arab

In 1929, an Arab force attacked the Jewish community (over 700 of them) in Hebron, Israel. According to one source, around 60 were killed and around 60 wounded. In Safed, Israel, shortly afterwards, 20 people were murdered and over 100 houses destroyed.

In 1948, following the Deir Yassin attack described above, and in retaliation, a convoy travelling under Red Cross badges to the isolated Jewish Hadassah Hospital and the Hebrew University was ambushed. Around 77 doctors, nurses, university students and teachers were killed.

Over the years, we have all become familiar with reports of rocket fire into Israeli towns and villages. There have also been many suicide bombings, although they have been mostly stopped at the present time by the security 'wall' (mostly a fence, but a concrete wall in some particularly vulnerable areas).

Randall Price, in his book 'Unholy War' (see Recommended Resources) describes the events leading up to the Palestinian Intifada which started in 2000. A visit to the Temple Mount by the then Israeli Prime Minister Ariel Sharon, during which he surveyed some Muslim construction work, was blamed. Sharon had stated it is the right of every Jew to visit the Temple Mount, following which a group of around 1,000 Arabs launched attacks.

The Palestinian Mufti preached an inflammatory sermon accusing the Israeli government of desecrating the Al-Aqsa Mosque on the Temple Mount. He called for Jihad to eliminate the Jews from Palestine. Hundreds of his congregation rushed onto the Temple Mount, fighting with the police and hurling down stones at the Jews who were praying at the Western Wall. Following this, violence erupted all over Israel.

In 2008 and 2009, there were attacks on motorists and pedestrians in Jerusalem by Arabs using two bulldozers and a car. There have been random shooting incidents such as the one in 2008 in a Jerusalem religious school and an attack on a bus full of children.

These later types of attacks are sometimes justified on the basis that they are born out of desperation and the Palestinians have no other choices. Such a view fails to take into account the bigger picture and Islamist 'martyr culture' - The idea of the dead suicide bomber being in Paradise with 72 virgins.

Occupation ?

We hear a lot about the 'occupation' of Palestinian lands but little about other disputes between nations over areas of land. To cite only two examples, Indian and Pakistan have been locked in argument over Kashmir for over 50 years, while a bitter feud has raged between the USA and Mexico over borders. How many people know about the border fence separating the two and all the problems it has caused?

Christian Arabs and Israel

There has been bitterness on the part of some Arabs and Jews due to the incidents I have mentioned and others. Jews and Arabs who become believers have to deal with this.

With reference to the Biram incident which I outlined, there is a difference in attitude between two different Arab believers that I have read of whose families were involved.

Elias Chacour, an Israeli Arab and a leader in the Melkite Church, is a former Biram resident. He has written a book in which he describes what happened and sets out his views on the historic and current situation in modern Israel. Unfortunately, there are few scriptural references in his book, which is largely anecdotal and emotive. His book boils down to an emphatic denial that the modern State of Israel is a fulfilment of Bible prophecy. Apart from a reference to his own interpretation of one of the Beatitudes, in my opinion he fails to build a scriptural case to support his view.

He rightly emphasises, in common with some other Christian authors, the need for Israel to be just and righteous. We need to pray that Israel looks to God and to the scriptures. It is clear that he does have a desire for Jewish/Arab reconciliation and, on a personal relational level, that may well be his strong point. However, the terms of reconciliation seem to be that the Jews accept that they have no more right to the Land than do the Arabs.

Arab Christian Riah Abu El-Assal, in his book *Caught In Between,* explains in chapter 11 how he formed a friendship with a kind friendly man he called 'Abuna', Arabic for 'Father' or Daddy'. The man's popular name was Abu Amar, better known to the world at large as the late Yasser Arafat! One of my daughters heard a Palestinian Christian woman at the UK Greenbelt Festival say that she does not believe that God ever told the Israelites to go into Canaan and dispossess and/or kill the Canaanites, because God wouldn't do that!

In contrast, another Arab believer is Yousef Dakwar, the pastor of a thriving Arab congregation based in Haifa in Israel. He also works closely with a believing Jewish congregation. Yousef's father was a Biram resident and he has, of course, told his children all about what happened and his sadness. This meant that Yousef grew up with a sense of bitterness towards the Jews and, when he came to faith in Jesus, the challenge was forgiveness. This was a struggle but he won through. *Unlike Elias Chacour, he fully accepts that the Jews have a covenant right to the Land.*[12] There are others like him both in Israel and in the Palestinian Territories.

See Appendix 4 for a powerful testimony of a Jewish Israeli believer about reconciliation with the Arabs.

Critics of Christian Zionism say that we are putting a stumbling block in the way of Muslim evangelism, not only in Israel but worldwide. *This we emphatically deny!* My Israeli pastor friends know pastors in the Arab nations who accept the Jews' Land Covenant and are seeing Muslims coming to faith. They teach them to love Israel.

There are some individuals and fellowships in Israel that are making real headway in bringing Arabs and Jews together in the Body of Christ, although my believing Israeli friends tell me it is a struggle. The majority of Arabs in Israel want to live in peace with Jews. Aviel Schneider, Editor of the Jerusalem-based magazine Israel Today, who has Palestinian friends, says *'On a personal level loving your enemies and reconciliation is possible; on a national level much harder…it is a mission to be accomplished by the Messiah and through his authority'…*[13]

Until recently, two of my closest friends were living in Jerusalem running Christchurch Guest House. Their workforce included Jews, Arabs and others and they were well aware of the difficulties faced by the Arabs. Those who live outside the boundaries of Israel and have to come through the checkpoints are often late for work.

Other Arabs and Israel

According to a recent issue of the UK-based Jewish Chronicle, the Saban Centre for Middle East Policy carried out a survey of Israeli Arabs. Some were clearly uneasy with their Israeli identity, and many said their rights in Israel are in decline. However, the survey did show that a clear majority of Israeli Arabs do *not* want to be part of a Palestinian state. They say that jobs and living standards are better in Israel than in the Palestinian Territories.

Israel Today magazine, on page 3 of their October 2009 issue, interview Nasreen Abdel Nabi, a Palestinian Arab resident of East Jerusalem. She says, amongst other things, *'I know many Palestinians who want to live under Israeli rule. They even wish they could serve in the Israeli police or army'* and *'we reject Palestinian President Mahmoud Abbas and his Palestinian Authority Government'*.

Each year, in the port city of Haifa in Israel, an event for the 275,000 population is held called 'Holiday of Holidays'. This encompasses Christmas, Hanukkah and Id al Adha. Hanukkah is a Jewish festival and Id al Adha is a Muslim one. This is not the sort of thing we hear about on world news.

Ishmael Khaldi is Israel's highest-ranking Muslim political advocate for the nation and is an Israeli Bedouin Arab. In response to hard-line critics of Israel, he says *'Israeli society is far from perfect…Israel's minorities fare far better than any other country in the Middle East…do Israel's Arab citizens suffer from disadvantage? You better believe it. Do African Americans 10 minutes from the Berkeley campus suffer from disadvantage?- you better believe it too…if Israel were an apartheid state, I would not have been appointed here, nor would I have chosen to take upon myself this duty…'* [14] He believes his people need to work with Israel for solutions to their problems.

There are two Arab pro-Israel websites listed in my Recommended Resources - Arabs For Israel and the Palestinian Zionist Organisation.

On the other side of the coin, the Israeli Parliament has a small number of Arab members who are sworn enemies of their *own* country.

Harsh Criticism of Israel

I have said elsewhere that I do not believe that Israel can do no wrong. However, we must ask why Israel, a democracy, attracts such massive worldwide attention and, at times, vitriolic criticism. We hear relatively little of tyrannical regimes such as Zimbabwe and North Korea. Also, the number of United Nations (UN) resolutions passed which are hostile towards Israel is out of all proportion in the framework of world affairs. According to Mitchell Bard, the General Assembly of the UN adopts 19 anti-Israel resolutions a year. [15]

Are Christian Zionists 'warmongers'?

Accusations of this nature abound in anti Christian Zionist literature, for example Professor Paul L. Maier in the forewords to Stephen Sizer's *Zion's Christian Soldiers* includes this misguided remark… *'to help Christians become the peacemakers they ought to be, rather than firebrands inflaming the world with wrongheaded ideas about the end times…'*

The short answer to the question is a resounding NO! These accusations are unjust and untrue. Of course we do not *want* war - who in their right mind would? I have friends who live in Israel, both Jews, Arabs and others. Would I *want* them to be injured or killed? Of course not and neither do I want Palestinians to be killed.

One of the regular prayer bulletins which I receive from Israel always ends with the exhortation *'pray for peace, prepare for war.'* In other words, we want peace but we are very aware of the reality of the situation concerning Israel. The hostility of many nations to Israel means that, at times, there seems no alternative but war. One characteristic of the wars in which Israel has become involved so far is that they have been mercifully short.

An Arab called Mosab Hassan Yousef, who is the son of a Hamas leader and was heading for a prominent role among Hamas himself, has become a Christian. He says *'You Jews should be aware: You will never, but never, have peace with Hamas. Islam, as the ideology that guides them, will not allow them to achieve a peace agreement with the Jews. They believe that tradition says that the Prophet Mohammed fought against the Jews and that therefore they must continue to fight them to the death.'* [16] Mosab has written a book called 'Son of Hamas'- See Recommended Resources.

There are, of course, many moderate Arabs and Arab groups who genuinely do want to live at peace with Israel. The question is, however, whose agenda will prevail- That of the moderates or that of the radicals?

In answer to prayer, God has often averted disaster in the fighting between the Arabs and the Jews, but it seems likely that there will be further conflicts. It seems to me that there will be at least one major war when all nations attack Jerusalem (see Zechariah chapters 12 to 14). Peace, in the end will be declared by the Prince of Peace Himself!

Christian Zionists are rightly sceptical of man-made political 'solutions' such as the USA-driven 'Road Map'. Those of us who see in the scriptures a future 'Anti Christ' ('anti' can mean 'instead of' rather than 'against') see him as a bringer of the most devastating false peace the world has ever known. Some say that if Northern Ireland's problems could be resolved, the Israeli-Palestinian ones can. This, however, overlooks some essential differences between the two scenarios.

Obviously peace negotiations can succeed temporarily, but they do not resolve the underlying issues. Only the Prince of Peace Himself will be able to bring in permanent peace in the Middle East. Some Christians say we should support peace initiatives from the United Nations and others, but this could include Jerusalem being divided and under international control. Jerusalem is mentioned over 600 times in the Bible but not once in the Koran- hardly a level playing field.

It has been said that the President of the Palestinian Authority ('PA'), Mahmoud Abbas, is a moderate. However, in a speech on 27 April 2009 in Ramallah, he said '*A Jewish state, what is that supposed to mean? You can call yourselves as you like, but I don't accept it and I say so publicly.*'[17] Speaking in Arabic, and recorded in the PA newspaper *Al-Hayat Al-Jadidia,* he has told other Arab leaders that he would support a war by Arab states against Israel. The Prime Minister of the PA, Salam Fayad, in an interview with Al-Arabiya TV said '*Israel can call itself whatever it wants, but the Palestinians will not recognise it as a Jewish state.*'[18]

Is the Lord always anti-war?
Try comparing the two following verses:

- Joel 3: 9-10 '*Proclaim ye this among the nations; prepare war; stir up the mighty men; let all the men of war draw near; let them come up. Beat your plowshares into swords, and your pruninghooks into spears...*'

- On the other hand, Micah 4:3 '*He will judge between many peoples and will settle disputes for strong nations far and wide. They will beat their swords into ploughshares and*

their spears into pruning hooks. Nation will not take
up sword against nation, nor will they train for war any more.'

It might look like the Lord can't make up His mind! Perhaps
the key lies in the wise words of Bishop Augustine of Hippo in
North Africa (AD 353 to 430) *'if we distinguish the times all*
scripture is in harmony with itself'.[19]

Chuck Cohen, in p 6 of the November/December 2009 issue
of Sword magazine says *'An increasingly accepted humanistic concept*
of God does not support the idea that He would fulfil His word by real
bloodshed, warfare and death. Yet how were we saved? Through the
*fulfilment of God's prophetic word in the shedding of Yeshua's (*Yeshua
means Jesus) *blood ending in his death, and only after that, through his*
resurrection'….

He goes on to list other examples from scripture, eg God
killed everyone but Noah and his family, Israel was set free
from Egypt partly by the death of all Egypt's firstborn, and
God led Joshua to conquer the Cannanites through warfare.

We are all longing for the 'swords into ploughshares' time but it will only
come about in God's time and in God's way! Many Christian
Zionists believe this will be in a future period of time known as
'The Millennium'. However, the United Nations in New York
has this scripture prominently displayed as if to say that it can
be engineered *now* by human effort.

Perhaps the constant threat of war is a factor in Israelis
turning to God. A recent *Ynet* poll in Israel found that 57% of
them are less optimistic about politics now than in 2000, but
more than one third said they have moved closer to God.[20]

Do Christian Zionists *unconditionally* support Israel?
Some 'anti Christian Zionist' writers unfairly tend to lump us
all into this category but, again, perhaps we haven't explained
ourselves properly. I would explain myself in this way:

I offer all Jews, whether living in Israel or not, unconditional
friendship (the same goes of course for the Arabs and

everyone else I come across). I want them to believe in Jesus, but if they won't, I will not withdraw friendship from them. I believe Israel has a right to exist as a sovereign nation and that Israel has been re-established by God according to his covenant promises. I also believe that both the secular and religious media misrepresent Israel, (including Evangelical publications.)

I therefore support Israel, but I do not necessarily agree with everything the Israeli authorities do. I do not like some aspects of Israeli society, amongst other things the very high abortion rate. My position broadly corresponds to that of many of my Christian Zionist friends. Unfortunately, there are some Christian Zionists who take extreme positions and have put some other Christians off a serious consideration of the important issues.

There are issues concerning justice in the Land of Israel, and between Israel and her neighbours. Justice is a very important biblical theme. If Israel commits injustices, we should not be afraid to speak out. Having said that, Canon Andrew White has also said *'Justice has come to mean 'Just what I want'. I don't even like mentioning the word, it's been abused by so many people with a political agenda.'* [21]

In my introduction, I said that I don't necessarily have a problem with pro-Palestinian groups unless they insist on putting the blame for all of the problems of the Palestinians on Israel. It is a tragedy that some Christian writers and speakers, who are rightly concerned about justice and the plight of the oppressed, are not as well informed on Israel as they could be.

As a result, they go along with incorrect accusations against Israel. Archbishop Desmond Tutu of South Africa and his inaccurate comparisons between Israel and South Africa (in its apartheid years) does not help the situation.

Let me end this chapter by emphasising that the primary warfare in and surrounding Israel is *spiritual* rather than

military.   The reasons for this will hopefully become clear in chapter 7.   Firstly, however, we will take a diversion in chapter 6 to look at some of the historical connections between Britain and Israel.

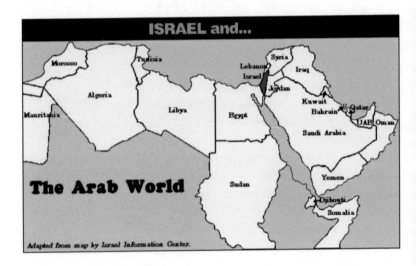

This map graphically illustrates the relative land areas of Israel and the surrounding, mainly Arab, countries. It can be found at http://www.jewishvirtuallibrary.org/jsource/Peace/arabworld.html

NOTES

1. Steve Maltz, *Land of Many Names,* p viii, Authentic Lifestyle 2003.
2. Ken Burnett, *Why Pray For Israel,* p 18, Marshall, Morgan & Scott 1983, ISBN 0 551 01042 8.

3. Richard Wolff, *Israel Today*, p 169, Tyndale House Publishers 1970, ISBN 8423 1810 0.

4. Eg Isaiah 14: 29-31 & Joel 3:4

5. Eg Matthew 2: 20

6. From an article *'The Promised Land'* in the Daily Express 8 May 2008.

7. Spoken at the celebration of the 10th anniversary of the Peres Peace Center in Israel in October 2008, reported in the January 2009 issue of Israel Today.

8. Mark Twain, *'The Innocents Abroad'*, New York 1966. I recommend a reading of his full report, quoted in Steve Maltz's booklet *'Plain Man's Guide to the Middle East Conflict'* and his book *The Land of Many Names*, Authentic Lifestyle, ISBN No 1-86024-287-1. These are both available from Christian Friends of Israel on 01323 410810, or go to www.cfi.org.uk

9. William Dawson, *'Modern Science in Bible Lands'*, New York 1890, pages 449-450.

10. Go to http://www.jewishvirtuallibrary.org/jsource/Quote/Weizmannq1.html

11. Elias Chacour , *Blood Brothers* , Kingsway Publications 1984, ISBN 0 86065 328 5.

12. Julia Fisher, *A Future for Israel*, ch 5, Authentic Media 2006, ISBN 1 86024 531 5.

13. Israel Today, July 2009 p 2.

14. From an article *'Lost in the blur of slogans'*- www.sfgate.com/cgi-bin/article.cgi?f=/c/a/2009/03/03/EDRP168GMT.DTL

15 From *'Israel and the UN- An Uneasy Relationship'*: www.jewishvirtuallibrary.org/jsource/UN/unisrael.html

16. From a report *Sound of the Shofar* # 80 from Eliyahu Ben-Haim, 11 August 2008 at www.b1149w.blu149.mail.live.com/mail/PrintShell.aspx?type=message&cpids=d841...

17. www.jta.org/news/article-print/2009/04/27/1004670/abbas-won-t-recognize-israel-as
18. www.israelnationalnews.com/News/News.aspx/124435
19. Sermon 32 on the New Testament.
20. Israel Today, March 2010 p 4..
21. Interview with Justin Brierley in 'Christianity' magazine, June 2009.

Recommended books
Myths & Facts by Mitchell G Bard - see Recommended Resources
Arabs in the Shadow of Israel by Tony Maalouf- see Recommended Resources

Chapter 6

Britain and Israel

In the late nineteenth century, a solicitor from Liverpool called William Quilliam converted to Islam and he opened Britain's first mosque in a house in Liverpool on Christmas Day 1889. Abdullah Quilliam, as he became known, was passionate for the cause of Islam and an influential man, bringing over a hundred relatives and friends into his new-found faith.

For Quilliam, this was just a start and he engaged in active plans to start a nationwide Islamic mission in Britain. He was promised financial and other support from powerful Muslim rulers. In 1908, he left England for a short trip abroad with the intention of returning to make a start on his plan. However, for some reason that the historical accounts do not record, he remained abroad for over twenty years and the plan never got off the ground. He died in 1932 a short while after his return to England. It seems to me that the hand of God was in those circumstances.

However, some decades later, Muslims started to come to the UK. A 2010 Barnabas Aid article entitled 'The Islamisation of the West' estimates the Muslim population of the UK at between 3 and 5 million. Mosques and Islamic academies are now rising all over the nation, accompanied by campaigns for the recognition of Muslim rights. In comparison, the rights of Christians in Muslim countries are often denied.

Why would God overrule Quilliam's plans and yet permit Islam to make ever-increasing advances in Britain in our day? Have we gone wrong somewhere?

I will return to this question later in this chapter but, for now, I have to deal with some important historical details from the seventeenth century onwards.

'Christian Zionism' is the legacy of the British Church

Christian Zionists in Britain have been accused by some other Christians of following novel ideas. This is rather ironic because the history of Christianity in Britain over several centuries leading up to the twentieth century shows that, far from following new ideas, Christian Zionists have actually *returned* to the beliefs and vision of their forefathers.

Many Christian leaders in Britain of yesteryear explicitly believed in and looked for the literal return of the Jews to the Land of Israel, in some cases seeking to hasten it. They simply accepted and proclaimed the prophetic scriptures, although they saw little, if any, tangible evidence of fulfilment in their day.

In contrast, too many British Christian leaders over the last sixty years or so have seemingly failed to grasp the significance of the events of the twentieth and twenty-first centuries.

John Wesley

John Wesley, if he were alive today, would surely rebuke them with his words from his commentary on Romans. He refers to chapter 11 and verse 12, saying '*So many prophecies refer to this grand event, that it is surprising any Christian can doubt of it*'. [1]

British support for a Jewish return to Israel

Britain came a long way, considering the stain on our past from the events of the Middle Ages. In 1290, we were the first nation to expel its Jewish population, giving rise to a wave of similar expulsions throughout Europe. Simon De Montfort, of my own home city of Leicester, was responsible for the first such expulsion from Britain.

He drew up a Charter (recently both spiritually and legally revoked), the effect of which was that no Jew should ever live in Leicester or its boundaries ever again.

In around 1650, a Jew named Menasseh Ben Israel pleaded with Oliver Cromwell for the re-admission of the Jews to England. This was on the ground that this was the means for achieving the Restoration of the Jews and the coming of the Messiah. Despite bitter opposition in the nation, his request was granted. Over several centuries after that, there was a growing swell of support in Britain for the return of the Jews to their land, eventually resulting in the famous *Balfour Declaration'* of 1917 (see later in this chapter).

The Vision *was* There

One writer who did a great deal of research and documented the development of thought and belief in Britain over the centuries leading up to 1948 was the late Franz Kobler. He was a Czech Jew born in Bohemia in 1882. He was a lawyer, author, historian, sociologist and psychologist. In 1956, he published a book called *'The Vision Was There'*, subtitled *'A History of the British Movement for the Restoration of the Jews to Palestine.*[2]

In page 7, in his preface, he states as follows:

> 'Nowhere more than in Britain has the idea of the Restoration of the Jews been developed into a doctrine and become the object of a movement extending over more than three centuries. Only in Britain the leading spokesmen of many generations have been inspired by the vision of a revived Israel. Only there the creation of a Jewish National Home has been a serious and almost continuous political issue which was finally translated into reality'.

Throughout the book, he lists the names of many prominent politicians, poets and authors, many of whom were believers, and many Christian leaders and hymnwriters. All of them had some sort of understanding of and vision for either the physical restoration of the Jews to the Land of Israel, their mass conversion to belief in Jesus as Messiah and Saviour, or both. They varied in their beliefs as to how and when these things would happen.

Some believed that the mass conversion of the Jews had to precede a national restoration to Israel, while others believed that the former would follow the latter. Still others did not consider that conversion was necessary as Christianity, in their view, did not displace Judaism.

I do not agree with all of the sentiments expressed by the people quoted in Kobler's book. However, there was an overwhelming sympathy for the Jews and a sense of a national, as well as individual, duty to help them end their days of exile among the nations.

A literal approach to the interpretation of Bible prophecies was common, in contrast to the tendency of many Christian leaders and theologians to adopt an allegorical or symbolic system of interpretation. I have commented on this in chapter 3.

It is interesting that, in the whole lengthy account given by Kobler, there is no mention at all of an anticipation of any difficulties with the Arabs concerning the prospect of a Jewish return to Palestine. However, problems with the Turkish administration of the region were expected.

The following are given as selected examples from Kobler's book and from other sources:

Two hymns, as examples of many written in the eighteenth century onwards.

Charles Wesley

'O that the chosen band might now their brethren bring,
And gathered out of every land, present to Zion's King!
Of all the ancient race not one be left behind,
But each, impelled by secret grace, his way to Canaan find.

We know it must be done, for God hath spoke the word;
All Israel shall their Saviour own, to their first state restored;
Rebuilt by His command, Jerusalem shall rise;
Her temple on Moriah stand again, and touch the skies.

Send then Thy servants forth, to call the Hebrews home;
From east and west and south and north, let all the wanderers come;
Where'er in lands unknown the fugitives remain,
Bid every creature help them on, Thy holy mount to gain.

William Cowper, a well-known 19th century hymn-writer and
friend of John Newton:

Oh Israel! of all nations most undone,
Thy diadem displaced, thy sceptre gone;
Cry aloud, thou that sittest in the dust,
Cry to the proud, the cruel, the unjust!
Knock at the gates of the nations, rouse their fears,
Say wrath is coming, and the storm appears,
But raise the shrillest cry in British ears!

The writings of Charles Haddon Spurgeon

In *Vol 17 pgs 703 & 704 of 'The Restoration and Conversion of the
Jews'*, he says:

> 'We do not think enough of it [ie the restoration of the
> Jews]. But certainly, if there is anything promised in

the Bible, it is this. I imagine that you cannot read the Bible without seeing clearly that there is to be an actual restoration of the children of Israel. "Thither they shall go up; they shall come with weeping unto Zion, and with supplications unto Jerusalem." May that happy day soon come! For when the Jews are restored, then the fullness of the Gentiles shall be gathered in; and as soon as they return, then Jesus will come upon Mount Zion to reign with his ancients gloriously'

Lord Shaftesbury and *William Wilberforce*, famous for their social reforms, were also ardent supporters of a restoration of the Jews to the Land of Israel. So were the famous poets *John Milton and Lord Byron*, and the novelist *George Elliot*.

I list at the end of this chapter recommended materials for further study in this area.[3]

I wonder why modern Christian writers such as Stephen Sizer and Colin Chapman think that we should reject the consistent testimony of the great Christian leaders of our nation of yesteryear and instead accept their version of events! Sizer visited Iran in 2007 where he assured Muslim clerics and leaders of nominal Christian denominations that Christian Zionists do not follow the historic teachings of the church.

He is partly correct in that there appears to be little, if any, support for a literal Jewish restoration, either in the period of the early Church Fathers, or in the Reformation period. However, as Kobler exhaustively illustrates, support grew in what has been called the 'Post- Reformation period (late sixteenth century onwards) for a restoration.

Twentieth Century
Coming to the 20th century, *Dr F B Meyer* was a great Evangelical preacher who founded a thriving church in Leicester. He also gathered national Christian leaders together in 1917 to form the Advent Testimony and Preparation

Movement (now the Prophetic Witness International). Their Manifesto stated that … *'the return of the Lord may be expected at any moment'*… *'Israel will be restored to their own land in unbelief, and afterwards converted by the manifestation of Christ as their Messiah'* and… *'under the reign of Christ there will be a further effusion of the Holy Spirit upon all flesh.'* [4]

Of course, we are not justified in returning to the beliefs of even such eminent men unless their beliefs were clearly rooted in the scriptures. I believe they were, but I encourage readers to investigate and verify this.

The 'Balfour Declaration' of 1917

Lord Arthur Balfour was the British Foreign Secretary in 1917 at the same time as David Lloyd George was Prime Minister. The main part of the Declaration read as follows:

> 'His Majesty's Government view with favour the establishment in Palestine of a national home for the Jewish people, and will use their best endeavours to facilitate the achievement of this object. It being clearly understood that nothing shall be done which may prejudice the civil and religious rights of existing non-Jewish communities in Palestine, or the rights and political status enjoyed by Jews in any other country'.

Shortly prior to the issue of the Declaration, Chaim Weizmann, a British Jewish chemist, had rescued Britain from probable defeat in World War 1 by inventing synthetic cordite. He was in return promised a homeland in Palestine for his people.

Rees Howells and his intercessors

No historical examination of contributions by British Christians to the restoration of the Jews to Israel would be complete without a mention of the unique part played by Rees

Howells and his team of intercessors at the Bible College of Wales.

During the Second World War, they prayed for five hours each evening, many after a day's work, often with periods of prayer and fasting during the day as well. Their prayers played a real part in the miraculous turning of the tide towards the end of the war.

Since 1938, Mr Howells had had a burden for the Jews to return to their land. In his own words *I firmly believe the times of the Gentiles are drawing to a close, and the Jews must be back in their own land when the Master returns.*[5] In October and November 1947, whole days were given to praying through for the return of the Jews to Palestine. He said *we pleaded that because of His covenant with Abraham 4000 years ago, God would take His people back to their Land, and Palestine should again become a Jewish State.*[5]

When the news came that the State of Israel was a fact, the College acclaimed it with rejoicing as *one of the greatest days for the Holy Ghost in the history of these 2000 years…now 4000 years after His covenant with Abraham, He has gathered all the nations together and made them give much of the land of Palestine back to them.*[5]

It is worth pointing out here that Mr Howells also said *God put me aside for some days to reveal the position of the Arabs… Just as we were only burdened for the Jews when we had to make intercession for them, so the Lord wanted us to have a concern for the Arabs also. They also are the sons of Abraham. Can the Holy Ghost bring in something which will break down the barrier between the Jews and Arabs that there may be a home and a blessing for both?*[5]

Unfortunately, the book by Norman Grubb which records all this does not give us any details of how Mr Howells saw that this might work out, but the ministries of reconciliation between Jew and Arab to which I have referred in chapter 5 are obviously a part of this.

A good book about God's dealings with the Arabs is 'Arabs in the Shadow of Israel' by Tony Maalouf- see Recommended Resources.

1917-1948: British inconsistency

The Balfour Declaration ushered in a period known as the 'British Mandate', ending four centuries of Turkish rule in Palestine. The League of Nations (later renamed the United Nations) awarded us the mandate and we were to implement the Declaration with 'close Jewish settlement in the Land'.

Britain practised political expediency and even treachery towards the Jews in appeasing the militant Arab nationalist movement in Palestine. In fact, we turned thousands of Jews away from the shores of Palestine in the 1930s and 1940s. The slippery slope Britain trod came to a head with a Government 'White Paper' in 1939 following which countless Jews, who might otherwise have found refuge in Palestine, perished in Hitler's 'Final Solution'.

On May 17 1939, Neville Chamberlain's government introduced the White Paper, which made the following provisions:

- An independent Arab State was to be set up in Palestine within ten years
- Only 75,000 Jews were to be admitted to Palestine during the next five years. After that, there would be no further Jewish immigration without the consent of the Arabs
- Only small parcels of land would be available to Jews

Some also believe that the British authorities knew more than they ever let on about what was going on in the concentration camps, but chose not to target the camps or the railway lines leading to them. After the war, the British authorities established camps for Jewish refugees in Cyprus and at Atlit in Israel. I have seen the one at Atlit, which has been preserved much as it was. Whereas I am not suggesting that the Jews were cruelly treated there, the layout is chillingly similar to the Nazi camps. This was at best insensitive.

There is no doubt that the Arabs were also frustrated by the ambivalence of the British authorities. Some of the outbreaks of violence on both the Jewish and Arab sides could perhaps have been prevented or reduced.

On 29 November 1947, the General Assembly of the United Nations voted on a resolution to divide Palestine into Jewish and Arab states. This was passed by 33 votes to 13 with 10 abstentions, one of which was Britain. The British authorities would not participate in the implementation of the Partition Plan and said they would withdraw fully by 15 May 1948.

On the evening of 14 May 1948, the State of Israel came into being and the British Mandate came to an end. Britain did not officially recognise the State of Israel until 29 January 1949.

British foreign policy towards Israel has not improved with the passing of time. The Foreign Office ('FO') usually goes with the Arab nations rather than Israel when it has to choose. The late Harold Wilson, one of our past Prime Ministers, said in his book 'The Chariot of Israel' that it is unfair to accuse the FO of having an inbuilt prejudice against Israel and the Jews. He says that it is just that, at any given time, there will be significantly more officials in the FO who have had experience in Arab countries than those with experience of Israel. I wonder if that is a good enough excuse.

Certainly a current proposal to remove Israeli sovereignty from over Jerusalem is much more likely to be vetoed by the USA than by Britain.

The sun sets on the British Empire
One of the consequences of Britain's 'about turn' appears to some of us to have been a loss of empire.

Ramon Bennett says:

> 'Britain is a dying empire. Her rapid decline is a forewarning of the cataclysm that is yet to come.

Those with a sense of nostalgia call her Great Britain, but she is no longer great- she is now just a part of Europe... Britain was a mighty power that reached to the ends of the earth, but she made the same mistake that so many other great world powers had made before her- she touched the apple of God's eye*'... (Zechariah 2:8)

*...'for whoever touches you (Israel) touches the apple of his eye- I will surely raise my hand against them so that their slaves will plunder them'...[6]

Clearly there were other contentious issues in the rise of the British Empire, such as slavery, racism and colonialism. However, my purpose here is solely to make a link between Britain's failure to act in accordance with the terms of her Mandate and the rapid decline of her Empire in the later twentieth century.

Derek Prince, quotes Isaiah 60:12 where, speaking of Israel, God says *For the nation or kingdom that will not serve you will perish; it will be utterly ruined*.

He goes on to say:

'In the 15th and 16th centuries, for example, Spain was the dominant nation of Europe, with a high level of culture, a powerful army and navy, and an empire that spanned both hemispheres. Within a century of expelling all Jews from her territories, Spain declined to a struggling, second-rate power'.

...Britain emerged victorious from two world wars, retaining intact an empire that was perhaps the most extensive in human history. But in 1947-48, as the mandatory power over Palestine, Britain opposed and attempted to thwart the rebirth of Israel as a sovereign nation.

From that very moment in history, Britain's empire underwent a process of decline and disintegration so rapid and total that it cannot be accounted for by merely the relevant political, military or economic factors.'...[7]

For a summary of the Empire's decline, see pages 202 to 211 of 'Teach yourself the British Empire' (Hodder Education ISBN 0-07-146148-5)

Not all Christians are convinced that the decline of the British Empire is a bad thing, but I see in it God's hand of judgment. If you do not agree, at least reflect on the fact that Britain's role as a missionary-sending nation has greatly reduced and God now has to send missionaries here from other countries to evangelise.

Is Israel the Key to UK Revival?

For some years, a conference has been running in England called 'Israel: Key to UK Revival', convened by an Assemblies of God pastor called Brenda Taylor. This is an account that was given by her a few years ago which I include with her kind permission and set out below for the consideration of the reader. The emphasis in italics is my own.

'The scene is Jerusalem; the day is Good Friday; the year is Jubilee. In the early hours of the morning, I was suddenly wide awake, and I saw a vision of the Israeli flag-i.e. a blue star on a white background. As I watched, it changed to a glittery silver/gold star on a black background.

The vision then began to take movement, and the star began to ascend into the night sky, and as it did, a comet trail of stardust was deposited and settled over the nations of the earth, which I recognized in the Spirit.

I asked the Lord what all this meant, and He spoke to my heart and said *'This is the time of Israel's ascendancy, and as she rises, it is time for the SETTLING of accounts with the nations. The deposit will remain for blessing or for curse, depending on how they have treated Israel.'*

I asked *'What of Britain?'* The answer was one I didn't want to hear, because the Lord said *'At this moment she is for curse'*. I felt so grieved inside, but immediately the Lord reassured me and said *'Don't be sad! It is a friend who warns, not an enemy. Where you can, take my message and encourage people to repent and to pray for My people Israel'*. The vision closed, leaving me with a burden for both Israel and the UK, and also a profound sense of the Lord's desire to be merciful if we'd humble ourselves and pray as He asked.

Following this, I discovered many of the reasons that Britain is for curse, including the forsaken promise of the Balfour Declaration. We had the mandate for modern Palestine and promised Israel its Bible land back. *We broke that promise before the ink was hardly dry, and took back 83%, leaving them with 17% of the original agreement.* Deuteronomy 27 states there is a curse for moving your neighbour's boundary mark, as well as the Genesis 12 curse for evil treatment of Israel.

When we broke the treaty, it divided the land of Israel with Islam, slicing off a huge chunk which was rightly theirs. I also discovered that it was British gunboats that blocked the Jews from returning to their homeland after the Holocaust. Britain also voted against Israel becoming a nation*, as well as cruel treatment when they were desperately in need of care after the war ended. From motivations of greed, we have befriended the Arabs at

Israel's expense. These are just some of the causes for the Lord's judgment on Britain.

At a later date, the Lord showed me the links between the root sin and the outworking of the curse. *Even as we sliced off Israel's land, so our Empire has been sliced off. Even as Britain divided the land of Israel with Islam, so He will divide Britain with Islam if there is no repentance. The division opened up the Jewish people to violence, bloodshed and unresolved disputes, and we have had horrendous problems in Northern Ireland along these same lines.*

There is much more that could be said, but we need to have an ear to hear what the Spirit is saying to the churches. The Church also needs to come to repentance for our history of bad feeling against the Jews. We have cut ourselves off from our roots, and although the root can survive without the branches, the branches cannot manage without the root.

Replacement Theology is totally against God's purposes as revealed in His Word, especially Romans 11, and this is seriously hindering the blessing God longs to pour out.

I pray for a deep and full revelation of God's heart on Israel, so that from a revived Church will come a Holy Spirit move in our nation that will bring a great end-time harvest'.

By Brenda Taylor

* *Author note*- actually, Britain abstained on the vote

It is significant that Brenda's earlier conferences were held at Bawtry Hall, which is the place where the strategy was formulated for the Battle of Britain in World War Two.

The Islamisation of Britain

Returning to the facts I set out at the beginning of this chapter about Quilliam's failed attempt to islamise Britain, a question must be asked- Is the steady rise of Islam in more recent times part of the Lord's judgments on us as a nation?

Some Christian leaders do not seem to share my concerns, for example Steve Bell of Interserve. In Christianity magazine, September 2008 p 10, there was a report of his talk at the 2008 Keswick Convention which includes this remark *'not only is an Islamic takeover in this country unlikely, but Bell also believes that the UK is providing a safe place in which Islam can change'*... I would like to think that Steve Bell is right, but something deep within me tells me he isn't.

Dr Patrick Sookdheo of the Barnabas Fund and the Institute for the Study of Islam & Christianity, in his foreword to David Pawson's book *'The Challenge of Islam to Christians'* [8] says *'Over the last hundred years, Islam has grown at a phenomenal rate. From a religion which seemed to have no future it is now vibrant, confident and assured... It is a part of the British landscape and is increasingly moving towards a position of dominance.'*

He does warn elsewhere, however, *'it is important that non-Muslim Britons should not succumb to alarmist, Islamophobic or racist trends'* and says *'Muslims in Britain are not a homogenous group, but represent a variety of national, ethnic, linguistic, sectarian and cultural backgrounds'.* [9] He acknowledges reform movements within Islam but warns that, when radical Islam is resurging, reform views are swept aside. Sometimes, radicals masquerade as moderates to gain influence.

The British are famous for 'tolerance'- A national trait that meant we were far from prepared for the Second World War. Hitler wasn't really a threat, he was just letting off steam! Prime Minister Neville Chamberlain returned triumphantly from his meeting with Hitler on 30 September 1938 proclaiming 'peace for our time'. Around sixty million lives were lost in the next seven years.

In the same way, we now hear many voices proclaiming Islam as a religion of peace. I wonder how familiar with the Koran such people are? President Barack Obama, in his quest for reconciliation between the USA and the Muslims, seems determined to present Islam as a religion of peace. Why? Is one of the reasons so that he can in time move to present Israel as the bad guys?

A piece of politically correct lunacy was the screening on Christmas Day 2008 by Channel 4 of an alternative Christmas message by the President of Iran, Holocaust-denier Mahmoud Ahmadinejad. He can be softly spoken and charming, but he is the leader of a government that wants enshrined in state law the death penalty for converting from Islam. He has said that Israel should be wiped off the planet.

The danger in Britain is that of ideological rather than military Jihad, although Patrick Sookdheo explains that military Jihad can be used in the final stages of a long-term campaign of ideological Jihad. Ideological Jihad is more subtle and cleverly concealed and many in our nation, both believers and unbelievers, seem to be deaf and blind to the relentless advances Islamists are making here.

The Archbishop of Canterbury, in 2008, said he thought some framework of Sharia Law might be helpful and Gordon Brown sees Islamic Banking as very desirable.

A report by the Christian Institute dated 30 June 2009 quotes think-tank 'Civitas' which says there are already 85 unofficial Sharia courts operating in the UK.

This does not, of course, mean to say that all individual Muslims and Muslim groups subscribe to a radical political agenda and nor does it detract from the need for us to love and befriend them, leading them to Christ. Many individual Muslims do want peace.

Rule Britannia, Britannia rules the waves, Britons never never never shall be slaves', we all once sang at the tops of our voices. I wonder!

Despite all I have said in this chapter, if we meet God's conditions He will move in power and may well stay the hand of Islam! A return to the faithful witness of our spiritual forefathers concerning Israel would certainly be helpful in resisting militant Islam in the UK. We need to cry out to God for the restoration of His favour on our nation!

Prospects of Revival in Britain

I doubt that it is a coincidence that some of those who take a more relaxed view of Islam in the UK are also lacking in a perception of God's restorative work with Israel. It seems to me that they fail to take sufficiently into account the enormous Islamic pressure against Israel. Some of them believe in Replacement Theology. Until they renounce it, a significant revival in the UK is unlikely in my view.

I put forward the suggestion that this is a factor in the lack of answers to the prayers of UK Christians for revival over some decades. I say this knowing that there are other factors involved, such as insufficient prayer, and that people do use the word 'revival' in different senses.

After all, surely there must be *some reason* why we have not seen a major move of God significantly affecting the unsaved in these islands since 1904! Is it a co-incidence that 1904 was before the time Britain started to lose the way in dealing with Israel?

Space does not permit me to refer in detail to all the moral and social problems of modern Britain but our decline is well advanced. Some may feel that the main stumbling block is the many bad laws passed particularly since 1960, but perhaps they are a consequence of something rather than its cause. Chuck Cohen of Jerusalem says that:

> 'although Jesus has set us free from the curse of breaking the law'…'the curse associated with denying God's promise to Abraham is still in effect- even for

believers- because it is an integral part of that promise. Is this one of the reasons why evangelism is a 'lost art' in the Church in the West and why the West is not experiencing revival such as we see in other parts of the world? Could this be the reason that much of what the West has called 'revival' since the early 1990's is very questionable at best, and more than likely deception...'?[10]

I do not feel that a global revival of immense proportions, as expected by some in our day, is likely to come without a meeting of God's conditions. One condition is to be in line with His Word concerning Israel. Having said that, I do not think there will *only* be apostasy and darkness. I go along with the view of the late Derek Prince who was once asked doesn't the Bible teach that things are going to get worse and worse. He replied that some things will get *worse* and other things will get *better*.

I outline the connection between the end-time salvation of Israel and 'revival' for all nations in chapter 7. What a great prospect! In chapter 3, I said that I doubt that, if the church in the early centuries had not lost its way to the extent that it did, Islam would ever have got off the ground. But it did and it is resurging in our day.

For now, Islam is a force to be reckoned with but I do believe that God has plans to bring it ultimately to an end.

NOTES

1. John Wesley's *Notes on the New Testament, London 1877*, p 236.
2. Available in full online at: www.britam.org/vision/koblercontents.html

3. 'The Destiny of Britain' and the 'Forsaken Promise' by Hugh Kitson, available on DVD from Hatikvah Film Trust at www.hatikvah.co.uk or call 0845 230 8788. Also short booklets: 'A Nation Called by God' and 'Are we on the edge of Judgement' published by 'Love Never Fails', PO Box 2687, Eastbourne, East Sussex BN22 7LZ. See also relevant resources supplied by Christian Friends of Israel, www.cfi.org.uk or call 01323 410810.

4. From In the Steps of F B Meyer by Colin Le Noury, page 20, Ambassador Publications 2007, ISBN 978-1-84030-185-4.

5. From 'Rees Howells, Intercessor', pages 244-245 by Norman Grubb, Lutterworth Press ISBN 0 7188 2046 0.

6. From Saga- Israel and the Demise of Nations, page 149, Arm of Salvation, Jerusalem.

7. From Last Word on the Middle East, pages 131 & 132, Derek Prince Ministries International.

8. Hodder and Stoughton, ISBN 0 340 86189 4, p xi.

9. 'Understanding Islamic Terrorism', Isaac Publishing, ISBN 0 9547835 0 6, page 7.

10. 'Grounded- the Promise of the Land in the New Testament'- available from Christian Friends of Israel- see note 3 above.

Recommendation

DVDs by Hatikvah Film Trust called 'The Destiny of Britain' & 'The Forsaken Promise'- see note 3 above.

Chapter 7

Not Israel for Israel's sake

I ended chapter 5 by saying that the warfare surrounding Israel is primarily *spiritual* rather than *military*. This chapter will look at some of the issues wrapped up in that statement.

Is Christian Zionism a 'cul-de sac'?

Some Christians are concerned that Christian Zionists have become sidetracked into a cul-de-sac and are obsessed with the destiny of one tiny nation to the exclusion of all other nations and issues. However, anyone who fits that description is well wide of the mark. It has always been in God's heart that Israel should bless and have the widest possible impact on the other nations.

Some of the people in the inter-church Prayer for Israel group that I have led in Leicester for some years have a broad perspective. When it comes, for example, to local outreaches to Gentiles, they are often heavily involved.

One of my Christian friends once said to me that he could not see why God would be so partial as to have a special place in His heart for the Jews. I replied that it is not a question of *partiality* but one of *purpose*. After all, doesn't God call many Gentile Christians and Christian organisations out for particular purposes, while we know that God loves us all equally?

Going back to God's original purpose in calling out the nation of Israel, those purposes have only ever been partly fulfilled and have been limited by disobedience. God, in Exodus 19:5-6, tells Moses to say to the people of Israel….'*Now if you obey me fully and keep my covenant, then out of all* nations you will be my treasured possession. *Although the whole earth is mine, you will be a kingdom of priests and a holy nation...*'

In Isaiah 60:3, God says to Israel *'Nations will come to your light, and kings to the brightness of your dawn....'*

Chapter 6 - about 'Britain and Israel' - told us of just a few of the many British Christians who, over some 300 years, looked for the Restoration of Israel. To some extent they did so because of the way that they understood the prophetic scriptures, but also because God had put a love for the Jews in their hearts. They *knew* that God's purposes with the Jews had yet to be completed.

Let us also look at a sample of other Christian leaders who have felt the same way:

Rheinhard Bonnke

The famous German evangelist gives an account on a tape about how God first called him to evangelise in Africa. He sought God in prayer before he ever went to Africa and all he heard from God, over and over again, was that he should pray for Israel! He said to the Lord that his concern was for Africa, not for Israel. He relates that God said to him *'pray for Israel and I will give you the world!'*

Adoniram Judson

He pioneered in Burma (now Myanmar) at a time when the gospel had never been heard in that country and founded the churches of the Karen tribe. However, before God released Adoniram to go to Burma, God set him aside for years to do nothing but intercede for the Jews. He then ministered in Burma for thirty-four years, involving great personal cost and suffering. Today more than one million Christians in that nation trace their spiritual roots to Adoniram Judson. [1]

George Mueller

He lived in the nineteenth century and came from Bristol. He is famous for his living by faith and his work in the establishment of orphanages and the scriptural instruction of the young in Britain. However, before he carried out his work with the orphanages, he was sent first to the Jews. He referred to them as *'God's chosen but erring people, Israel.'* [2]

Opportunities opened up for Mueller to work among the Jews of London. He worked firstly with the London Society For Promoting Christianity Amongst the Jews (now CMJ- The Church's Ministry Among Jewish People). He later worked on his own. In his interview with the London Society, Mueller described the words spoken to him as *'like fire within him.'* [2]

To the Jew First

All the above people honoured the principle of Romans 1:16 *'for I am not ashamed of the gospel; for it is the power of God unto salvation to everyone that believes; to the Jew first, and also to the Greek'...* If you read the book of Acts carefully, you will see that the normal pattern was that the gospel was proclaimed first in Jewish gathering places. This carried on *even after* Paul and Barnabas, in Acts 13:46, declared that the Jews had judged themselves unworthy of eternal life and that they would turn to the Gentiles. Everywhere they went, they still went first to the synagogue and the results were that large numbers of both Jews and Gentiles came to faith.

There has been some application of the 'to the Jew first' principle since the book of Acts. In chapter 4, I mentioned John Wilkinson's book 'God's Plan For The Jew'. He says *'wherever Jews are to be found in towns and cities to which missionaries are sent, let the apostolic order be observed, "to the Jew first, and also to the Gentile."'* [3] Some argue that the priority of the gospel to the Jew was only first in time, not in importance. Others, such as Wilkinson, say that it is a permanent divine order. The Greek word *proton* translated 'first' can mean either first in time, first in importance, or both.

The fact is that God has never given up on his original purpose for Israel and there is much yet to be outworked.

Before coming to the main theme of this chapter, it is necessary to refute an ill-informed criticism of Christian Zionists.

Do Christian Zionists evangelise Jews?

Christian Zionists today are sometimes accused 'en masse' of not preaching the gospel to the Jews, i.e. we are only concerned with supporting the State of Israel. This is a misleading generalisation. There are organisations and many individuals sharing the gospel with the Jews at the rate of thousands each year. Two examples are The Church's Ministry Among Jewish People (CMJ) and Jews for Jesus.

However, some Christian Zionist organisations who assist with helping Jews emigrate to Israel do have an agreement with the Israeli authorities not to evangelise the Jews they take to Israel. Some Christians have vehemently criticised this policy, although there is evidence of some Jews later coming to faith owing to the love shown them by staff and volunteers of these organisations.

I turn now to the consummation of God's purposes for Israel.

The Future of The Jews

I strongly recommend a careful reading of Romans chapters 9 to 11. I now highlight a few aspects of Romans 11 to show that the main reasons for emphasising God's dealings with Israel are far-ranging ones.

In chapters 1 to 8 of Romans, Paul does not deal with Israel, but deals with individual believers, making specific points about the Jews. He then turns to a consideration of Israel *as a nation*.

There are many significant statements made in chapters 9 to 11 about Israel but the two I will draw attention to and link together are in chapter 11:

1. Verse 15: *'For if their* rejection is the reconciliation of the world, what will their* acceptance be but life from the dead?'*

* see the previous verse- Paul, a Jew, is speaking of his 'own people'

2. Verses 26-27 *'And so all Israel will be saved, as it is written:' The deliverer will come from Zion; he will turn godlessness away from Jacob, and this is my covenant with them when I take away their sins'*....

I will deal with these in reverse order as we need to be clear about who the 'Israel' spoken of in verses 25-27 actually is.

'All Israel will be saved'

These verses have to be considered in their context and in the whole flow of chapters 9 to 11 of Romans. The opening verses of chapter 9 remove any possibility of arguing that 'Israel' in these chapters means 'The Church'. Paul refers in 9:3 to *'those of my own race, the people of Israel'*. There is only one verse in all three chapters where he uses the word 'Israel' to mean anything different. That is 9:6, where he uses it in the sense of a true 'Israel', or a holy remnant.

The term 'all Israel' in 11:26 has been interpreted in a number of different ways by different commentators. I set out below some of those views with my comments:

'Israel' means 'The Church'
I have dealt with this in chapter 3 and above.

'All Israel' means all Jews who have ever lived

This would mean that salvation, for the Jew, is based on their racial covenants with God, and not through faith and righteousness. The sacrifice of Jesus would be unnecessary for them. This is known as 'Two Covenant Theology' or 'Dual Covenant Theology' and is as much an error as is Replacement Theology. The Episcopal and Presbyterian denominations in the USA appear to have been influenced by this teaching and US Christian leaders John Hagee and Pat Robertson are reputed to be in favour of it.

'All Israel' means the 'Elect of all the Ages'

This view seems to have come from the writings of some of the Reformers. Some Evangelicals seem to feel that everything the Reformers did and said must have been right. Much as I honour them for their courage and their tenacity in opposing false religion, they were not right about everything. Nor did they understand all scriptural truth.

In their view, 'Israel' in verse 25 and in some other places means the Jews, or ethnic Israel. However, in verse 26 'all Israel' to them means 'The Elect of all the Ages'. By this, they mean faithful Jews who lived before Christ plus Christians, both Jewish and Gentile.

Their view, in my opinion, fails to explain the significance of the *'hardening in part'* (11:25) which has temporarily come on Israel *'until the full number of the Gentiles has come in'* (11:25). It also seems to me to have a very strange logic behind it and to ignore the connection between this passage and Jeremiah 31, from which Paul is quoting.

The quotation from the 'Old' Testament in verses 26-27 is full of terms which are frequently used in the Bible to stand for Israel in the simple racial sense and is inextricably linked with verse 26. Has 'Israel' changed meaning again?

We also have to ask the question who are the enemies of the gospel spoken of in verse 28? Is that also the 'elect of all the ages'- or is it *racial* Israel? Is Paul then merely saying that 'all the saved will be saved' and that the 'elect of all the ages' are enemies of the gospel? Surely that is nonsense. I doubt that Paul would have used the doxology in verses 33 to 36 if that is his meaning.

This view violates the whole context and flow of chapters 9 to 11. As Paul starts chapter 10 by saying that *'my heart's desire and prayer to God for the Israelites is that they may be saved'*, it is unlikely that the meaning of *'all Israel will be saved'* has a different application. As John Murray has said in his comments on Romans in the *New International Commentary on the New Testament (Vol 2 p 96, Eerdmans 1959-65), 'it is exegetically impossible to give to "Israel" in this verse any other denotation than that which belongs to the term throughout this chapter'.*

In my view, 'All Israel will be saved' refers to a significant proportion of a particular generation of Jews coming to faith in Jesus.

In my opinion, the term *'all Israel'* is most likely a figure of speech known as a *'synecdoche'*(pronounced *sin eck dok ee).* This is the use of a term meaning most, rather than all, of a particular class or group. It is used frequently in the Bible, for example in Matthew 2:3 where we read... *'when King Herod heard this he was disturbed, and all Jerusalem with him.'*

This interpretation is in keeping with the good general guideline of comparing scripture with scripture in order to arrive at a correct understanding.

Of the commentators who favour this interpretation, ie of a mass conversion of Jews at a particular point in time, some also believe in the physical restoration of Israel in the Land. Others do not see that as necessary or desirable and place emphasis on the absence of detail on this topic in the New Testament. I have dealt with this in chapter 4. My view is that the prophetic scriptures indicate that God will deal in a particular way with the Jews *in the Land.*

Historically, there has always been a small remnant of Jewish Christians but now we are seeing the beginnings of a national move of the Holy Spirit in Israel. Since the establishment of the modern State of Israel, there has been a gradual increase in the number of Israelis coming to faith. There has been a corresponding increase in the number of congregations of 'Messianic Jews' or 'Hebrew Christians', or whatever term you may use to describe them. In Israel in 2007, I came across an entire coach load of believers from one town. 20 years or so ago, you would have been hard-pressed to find a few of them. Groups of mainly secular Jews from communities called Kibbutzim have been visiting a large congregation of believers in Haifa, to find out what they believe and practice.

In the Israeli Parliament, there is now a monthly Bible Study held, albeit 'Old' Testament only.

This is only the 'tip of the iceberg' in terms of what is going on in Israel in terms of evangelism and is not what we hear about via the media. As well as now evangelising their own people in Hebrew, certain groups of Israeli believers are beginning to send out teams to other nations. Many different languages are spoken by Israeli Jews and they are familiar with many cultures. What a base for a formidable missionary force once they are sealed with the Spirit of God!

Paul's prediction in verses 26-27 of Romans 11 ties in with the words of the prophets about God's cleansing of Israel in various prophetic passages. See Ezekiel 36:24-32; Zechariah 12:10-14 and 13:1-2 and Isaiah 4.

In Matthew 23:39, Jesus said to Jews in Jerusalem... *'you will not see me again until you say "Blessed is he who comes in the name of the Lord..."* This links with the coming return of Jesus to Jerusalem (see Zechariah 14:4 and Acts 1:11) and a reversal of the historic rejection of him as Messiah by his own people. Jerusalem is a massively important place biblically. It is:

- the ancient seat of the Davidic Kingdom
- the place where Jesus died and rose again
- the place where the church began
- the place where Jesus is coming back to
- the place where Jesus will rule from

Having looked at the meaning of the term 'All Israel' and noted the forthcoming major move of the Holy Spirit in Israel, we can now look at the effect that it will have on the rest of the world - *Life from the dead.*

An Evangelist's dream

Have you ever wondered why spreading the gospel seems such hard work and why the results of a lot of evangelistic events are disproportionate to the time and effort going into them? Adrian Plass, in his book 'Bacon Sandwiches *and S*alvation' (An A-Z of the Christian Life) jokingly gives us the following definition of the phrase: *'The Lord will bring the ones He wants':* *'desperate phrase sometimes employed by those responsible for a badly-organised, poorly advertised, underfinanced, low quality Christian event for which only thirteen tickets have been sold in total'.* [4]

Christian missionaries do a great job and the Lord uses them, but they battle against ill-health, language difficulties and other obstacles and distractions. This is no criticism of them, but missionaries sometimes return home feeling defeated. All this sometimes makes you wonder.

Of course there are all sorts of different aspects of this, such as the obvious fact that human nature fights God, and the cultural and other obstacles facing missionaries. Then there is the fear of evangelism many Christians seem to have and so on.

However, going back to my comments earlier in this chapter about Romans 1:16, I am convinced that the gospel would up to now have made more progress if the 'to the Jew first' principle had always been honoured. Having said that, we can look forward to better things because linked to the 'all Israel will be saved' of verse 26 is the 'life from the dead' of verse 15.

'Life from the dead'

God did not choose Israel for Israel's sake. Romans 11 paints a picture of a spiritually-restored Israel leading to a spiritually-resurrected world, e.g. verse 12 *'but if their transgression means riches for the world, and their loss means riches for the Gentiles; how much greater riches will their fullness bring?...'*

In the 19th century, in London, there was a society created known then as the London Society for the Promotion of Christianity amongst the Jews.[5] One of its leaders was the Rev Charles Simeon, a prominent national Evangelical Anglican leader of the time. Giving an address at one of the meetings, he concluded by saying that they had met together that day *'for the furtherance of the most important object in the world, viz., the conversion of the Jews.'*

When he sat down, a sceptic in the congregation named Edward Bickersteth wrote on a slip of paper-*'Eight million Jews, eight hundred million heathens; which of these is the most important?'* This paper he handed to Simeon, who at once turned it over and wrote on the other side: *'Yes, but if the eight million Jews are to be as life from the dead to the eight hundred million heathens- What then?'* Bickersteth went on to preach at 18 anniversary meetings of the Society.

The effects of Israel's National Salvation

There are many passages in the Bible that show us that there will be a glorious age yet to come in which Israel will have a prominent place and will bless the other nations in many ways. I will quote two and list a few more that can be looked up.

- Isaiah 27:6 *'In days to come Jacob will take root, Israel will bud and blossom and fill all the world with fruit.'*[6]

- Isaiah 52:9-10…. *'Burst into songs of joy together, you ruins of Jerusalem[6], for the Lord has comforted his people, he has redeemed Jerusalem.[6] The Lord will lay bare his holy arm in the sight of all the nations, and all the ends of the earth will see the salvation of our God.'*

- See also Isaiah 19 and 66:10-13; Zechariah 14:16-21; Micah 4:1-5.

? The Fall of Islam ?

I realise that I am now in danger of seeming to contradict what I set out in chapter 6 about the rise of Islam in Britain. Sometimes though we need to look at the picture that is right in front of us and, at the same time, look to see what is on the far horizon. In terms of what I am about to say now, although the picture with Islam in Britain gives rise to very serious concern, we can take encouragement and hope from our expectation of what God will ultimately do.

I see, as one of the likely effects of Romans 11, the salvation of millions of Muslims, or former Muslims as they will be by then. John Wesley also thought so and he comments on verse 12 as follows …*'So many prophecies refer to this grand event, that it is surprising any Christian can doubt of it. And these are greatly confirmed by the wonderful preservation of the Jews as a distinct people to this day. When it is accomplished, it will be so strong a demonstration, both of the Old and New Testament revelation, as will doubtless convince many thousand Deists, in countries nominally Christian… And this will be a means of swiftly propagating the gospel among Mahometans and Pagans; who would probably have received it long ago, had they conversed only with real Christians.'* [7]

The senior pastor of Carmel Assembly in Haifa, Israel, David Davis, knows Arab pastors in Israel and the surrounding nations. He tells in his newsletters and his book 'The Elijah

119

Legacy' of the moving of the Holy Spirit and the many conversions amongst Muslims that are already taking place. In his chapter 'The Rise and Fall of Islam' he says *Before Jesus returns, Islam will fall and the Lord will sweep millions of former Muslims into His kingdom. It is beginning to happen in Kosovo, Indonesia, Mozambique, Uganda, Nigeria and Afghanistan.*[8]

Lance Lambert, a Jerusalem-based Bible Teacher, gave a prophecy on 20 August 2006, part of which said… *'I will also reap a huge harvest out of Islam, in the day that I will break its power… Young men and young women in multitudes will come out of Islam, saved by my grace and filled and anointed by my Spirit…'*[9]

Could there be more in the words of Jesus that 'salvation is of the Jews' (John 4:22) than we have realised so far?

? End Time Global Revival ?

There have been many predictions in recent times of a great global revival occurring before the return of Christ. There is, it seems to me, an unnecessary polarisation. On the one hand, all sorts of extravagant claims are made as soon as there is a flurry of apparently successful 'revival meetings'.

On the other hand, some put a strong emphasis on a great falling away and deception in the church. The 'either/or' mentality of the church strikes again (see chapter 2). The scriptures speak of *both* an apostasy *and* an end-time harvest.

As far as I can see, the only specific predictions of a final worldwide revival in the Bible are those that are specifically linked to the national salvation of Israel and its aftermath.

We all long for the evils of this present world system to come to an end. Many of us work in various ways towards that. I believe that to support God's purposes for Israel is to hasten the final outpouring of the Holy Spirit and the return of the Lord Jesus that we long for.

What about the 'End Times'?

Does a belief in this kind of future for Israel and the rest of the world mean that I have to stick to a particular dogma about the order of events in the end times? The short answer is no.

People sadly sometimes fall out over 'eschatology', the doctrines of the End Times. Certain rather daunting theological terms have been invented, for example *'dispensationalist', 'pre-millennial', 'pre-tribulation rapture'* and so on. If you don't understand the terms I am using, don't worry about it.

Some have suggested that teaching on Bible Prophecy should be thrown out of the church altogether, on the basis that it is divisive. However, this would mean that we are ignoring some 25% of the content of the Bible!

I believe that the study of Bible prophecy is a rewarding one although this is not the place to go into it all. The fact of the matter is that one does not have to belong to a strictly defined school of thought to believe that God has a distinct purpose and a glorious future for the Jews. You don't have to be a 'Dispensationalist' or necessarily believe in a 'Rapture' followed by the seven year 'Tribulation', although many Christian Zionists do.

Many Christian Zionists believe in a literal 1000 year period yet to begin called the Millennium, in which Jesus reigns over the earth from Jerusalem with Israel having a prominent role. However, some of the great Christian leaders of our nation in bygone days who looked for the restoration of Israel (see chapter 6) had differing views on this issue.

Will the church meet Jesus in the air before, in the middle of, or after the 'Great Tribulation'? Again, there are Christian Zionists in all three camps and some persuasive arguments for all three positions.

CMJ, one of the leading Christian organisations working with the Jews, does not have a dogmatic stance on the prophetic scheme of end time events.

What we *can* be absolutely certain about from the scriptures is that, however things pan out, the Jews have a critical role.

Let us ask the question- why has the Second Coming of Jesus been delayed for so long? The gospel has not yet been preached to every nation (Matthew 24:14) and the Jews are still not ready as a people to receive Him. Let us speed on their preparation!

Chosen, but not willing?

Just to finish this chapter, something from my personal experiences of visiting Israel:

I was swimming with my family at the 'Hot Springs' in the Galilee area of Israel some years ago and I remember looking round at the local people who were there. I was thinking that I could not imagine a bunch of people who looked *less likely* to become what God says in His Word they will become. Many of them just aren't interested right now.

Many Jews would rather God hadn't chosen them- A sort of 'go and choose someone else' attitude. **But God's word will not return to him empty (Isaiah 55:11).**

At the end of the day, it's all about God's name and His glory! *Therefore say to the house of Israel, "This is what the Sovereign Lord says: It is not for your sake, O house of Israel, that I am going to do these things, but for the sake of my holy name, which you have profaned among the nations where you have gone."*[10]

NOTES

1. Philip Yancey, *Rumours of Another World*, Zondervan 2003, p 214, and John Waters '*Storming the Golden Kingdom*', Send the Light 1989.

2. Sources- '*George Mueller of Bristol*' by Dr A T Pierson, Pickering & Inglis Ltd, 1972; ps 34-35, 50, 57 and extracts from Mueller's journal at www.gutenberg.org/files/20379/20379.

3. John Wilkinson, *God's Plan for the Jews,* Paternoster Press 1946, p 75.

4. Authentic Media 2007, ps 175-176

5. Among the chief patrons of the new society were Lord Shaftesbury and William Wilberforce MP. It is now known as CMJ. This is active in the UK, Israel and elsewhere.

6. In this verse, 'Jacob' and 'Israel' mean the same thing. In the Bible, the terms 'Jacob', 'Zion', and even sometimes 'Jerusalem' can mean simply 'Israel'.

7. *Explanatory notes on the New Testament* by John Wesley, London 1877, p 236.

8. *The Elijah Legacy* by David Davis, Thomas Nelson 2003, p 230. The chapter in which this quote is included is also available separately called 'The Rise and Fall of Islam'- go to www.carmel-assembly.org.il

9. For the whole prophecy, go to www.lancelambert.org/prophetic5.html

10. Ezekiel 36:22.

Epilogue

I leave it to the reader to reflect on all I have said and hopefully be motivated to do some further study on the subjects I have introduced.

To those who remain sceptical or just uncertain, I say just remain open and ask the Lord to guide your thoughts.

To those who have found this book at all convincing, I point out that a response is required, as well as further study. Teaching about Israel can be very interesting, but it must not remain purely cerebral. It needs to move from our heads to our hearts. My own experience, as an avid reader and student, has been that I started off by reconsidering Israel on a scriptural basis. I became mentally convinced of truth which I had not previously understood. However, this was not enough and when I first went to my church's Prayer for Israel Group ('PFI'), I found that I could not pray for the Jews, try as I may.

It seemed there was a spiritual barrier that I needed to break through and I had no warmth of heart, so I asked the Lord to give me supernaturally a love for the Jews. He did so and it was a powerful and profound experience. I then could hardly get through a PFI meeting without crying, although that later levelled out.

In essence, the required response is twofold involving both prayer and practical action. The level of commitment will vary from person to person and we must all listen to the Lord on this.

My suggestions for consideration are:

- Join a prayer group if one exists in your area, eg 'Prayer For Israel' or the 'Ebenezer Emergency Fund'.

- Consult one or more of the various Christian organisations connected with Israel- See list in Recommended Resources.
- Consider supporting one or more of those organisations financially (*Romans 15:27… 'For if the Gentiles have shared in the Jews' spiritual blessings, they owe it to the Jews to share with them their material blessings'…*)
- Go to meetings and/or conferences on Israel in your area.
- Some may be called to support Christian organisations that help Jews to emigrate to Israel (known as 'making Aliyah'). See Recommended Resources. Some Christians feel it right to financially contribute to Aliyah, others do not.

Some may be in a position to do more and could get involved with one of the organisations, either on a paid or voluntary basis. A word of caution here is in order. Sometimes, those who help Jews make Aliyah enter into an agreement with the Jewish authorities not to evangelise them on the voyages to Israel. It is not my intention to judge them for such agreements but, in my view, they should be the exception and not the rule - Romans 1: 16 says that the gospel is first to the Jew.

There are many opportunities in Israel for Christians to go and serve in various ways as temporary volunteers. This could be anything from a few weeks to a few years.

When giving money we should as far as possible check that none of it is likely to end up in the hands of Jewish organisations in Israel that are in direct opposition to Jewish evangelism.

Some may be called, as I am, to help other Christians to understand about Israel and to make use of the available resources. An important area also is to gain an understanding of Christianity's Jewish roots, which have been largely lost. This is beyond the scope of this introductory book.

A cautionary word on praying. Many people quote from Psalm 122 – *'Pray for the peace of Jerusalem',* but not everyone knows how to go about it. This is why I recommend joining a prayer group, even if you only go from time to time. Prayer for Jerusalem must be focussed and specific rather than just *'Lord stop the killing',* desirable as that is.

Examples of aspects to focus on are:

- Israel's security and Defence Forces
- Israel's salvation
- Christian workers in Israel
- Jewish and Arab fellowships and ministries
- Israel's Government
- Israel's 'Interior Ministry' and its anti-missionary focus
- Aliyah

And last, but certainly not least, *go* to Israel! - Either on a tour or under your own steam. If you are not sure how to choose a tour, please feel free to contact me at theheartofthematter.co.uk

Appendix 1

Statement of Purpose of the Leicester Prayer For Israel Group

I wrote this after a conversation I had in the early 2000s with a former member of my church. He was someone I knew did not share my perceptions and I asked him to tell me clearly and honestly how he saw the Prayer For Israel Group.

The call to pray for Israel stems from the following:

- God's choosing of the Jews as His first covenant people as their falling away from grace is clearly explained in Romans 9 to 11 as only temporary.

- A recognition of the fulfilment of Biblical Prophecy in the ongoing re-gathering of the Jews to their ancient promised homeland. We desire to see them in a position where the veil is removed from their minds and they recognise their Messiah, Jesus, who was sent first to the House of Israel.

- An understanding firstly that the Gentiles who have been grafted into God's people through the Jewish Messiah owe a debt to the Jews. Secondly that the issue of God's blessings on the Church is linked with the attitude of the Church to Israel.

Some important points about the group are:

- A Prayer For Israel group is not a collection of people who believe that the Israelis can do no wrong, although occasionally I have met such people. Wrong decisions are made and injustices committed by Israel. On the other hand, a disproportionate amount of blame for the controversies that arise is often attached to Israel by biased media reporting.

- Those who pray for Israel do *not* have a racial bias against Arabs. Our praying should include them and Israel should, biblically, be hospitable to the 'stranger' in the nation. Again, however, it must be borne in mind that there are still Muslim groups who remain committed to the removal of Jewish sovereignty from the Land of Israel. In some cases, they desire the entire destruction of the Jewish race.

- It is *not* the belief of the Prayer For Israel group that there are two ways of salvation - i.e. one for Jews and one for Gentiles. Paul speaks in Romans 11:25 of a day coming when all Israel will be saved. However, he does not mean that the need to come to God through Jesus and the cross will be bypassed in some way.

By David Evans, on behalf of the Leicester PFI Group

Appendix 2

Hints on praying for Israel

Prayer for Israel is not common practice in most churches. Sometimes this is because Israel is regarded as just one nation among others. Or it is the Palestinians that favour our prayers? Are they not the oppressed that the church is called to support? More and more we hear the argument that one can only pray for Israel if this is in balance with our prayer for the Palestinians.

I call this an attempt for politically correct prayer. However, prayer is not about our judgement concerning who is right and who is not. There are many nations who oppress their subjects. Some oppress other nations economically to keep up a certain standard of living for themselves... Which nation can escape God's judgement? Indeed, we need to pray for the nations! But our prayers are not meant to reflect our politically correct judgements. Prayer is our response to the call from God to join Him preparing the coming of His kingdom. And the king of the Jews heads His kingdom. Remember what was written above the cross of Jesus? "Jesus of Nazareth, king of the Jews"

Let us not be inspired through what the media tell us about the aggressor and the victim. Let us first of all be moved by God's Word. There we read that Israel is part of His strategy to reach the nations. Jesus said to the Jews "you will not see me again until you say, 'Blessed is he who comes in the name of the Lord.'"

Praying for Israel is praying for the coming of His kingdom. It has nothing to do with our politically correct judgements, but with joining the moving of God's Spirit.

Let us pray for Israel!

Gilbert Lammerts van Bueren, October 2009

(From the website of Near East Ministry, a ministry serving Arabs and Jews)

Recommended books:

Praying for the Peace of Jerusalem by Penny Valentine, Tahilla Press 2004, ISBN 978-1842911872

Praying for Israel and the Arab Nations by Penny Valentine-Tahilla Press, contact pennyprayer@googlemail.com

Major issues faced by Israel in conflicts

When Israel is involved in international conflicts, media bias against Israel is often at its worst.

The following summary should be read in light of the fact that the three most often-repeated accusations against Israel, during and after times of armed conflict, are that Israel:

- Is in 'clear violation' of International Law
- Deliberately targets civilians
- Responds 'disproportionately' to aggression

Here are some extracts from a series of presentations given by a number of lawyers and others on 18 June 2009 about the Israeli operation in Gaza in 2008/09, to the Jerusalem Center for Public Affairs. The issues highlighted are typical of other conflicts in which Israel has been engaged- e.g. the 2006 Lebanon War.

Most of the speakers concluded that Israel does not do enough, or act quickly enough, in conflict situations to ensure that the true facts get to the media.

Daniel Taub, Director, General Law Division, Ministry of Foreign Affairs, Israel

'During the Gaza War, the conditions were particularly complex due to Hamas' violation of international humanitarian law. Examples included dressing as civilians, using human shields, placing rockets among the civilian population, and booby traps in residential areas.'

Pnina Sharvit-Baruch, Law Faculty, Tel Aviv University, Former Head of International Law Department, Military Advocate General's Office
'International law is flexible and adapts itself to changes in the world. It is based on practices of countries in the international community…there is flexibility in every law. One example is the law of proportionality. This principle is very flexible. There is a balance between reality and the goal of the mission.'

Colonel Richard Kemp, CBE, Former Commander of the British Forces in Afghanistan
'…the battlefield- in any kind of war- is a place of confusion and chaos, of fast-moving action…the fog of war, sometimes literally fog, but always fog in the sense of chaos and confusion means that mistakes are made… we must not confuse mistakes made as a genuine consequence of the chaos and fog of war with deliberate defiance of rules of engagement and the laws of war. Mistakes are not war crimes'.

'Enemy forces sometimes adopt the other side's uniforms as a deception or ruse. But in the type of conflict that the Israeli Defence Forces recently fought in Gaza and Lebanon, and Britain and America are still fighting in Iraq and Afghanistan, these age-old confusions and complexities are made one hundred times worse by the fighting policies and techniques of the enemy…'

'Do these Islamist fighting groups ignore the international laws of armed conflict? They do not… Instead, they study it carefully and they understand it well. They know that a British or Israeli commander and his men are bound by international law and the rules of engagement that flow from it. They then do their utmost to exploit what they view as one of their enemy's main weaknesses.'

'Hamas of course deployed suicide attackers in Gaza, including women and children. Women and children are trained and equipped to fight, collect intelligence and ferry

134

arms and ammunition between battles'…They also ordered, forced when necessary, men, women and children, from their own population, to stay put in places they knew were about to be attacked by the IDF…'

'…Hamas, like Hizbollah, are also highly expert at driving the media agenda. They will always have people ready to give interviews condemning Israeli forces for war crimes. They are adept at staging and distorting incidents.'

'When possible the IDF gave at least four hour's notice to civilians to leave areas targeted for attack.'

'During the conflict, the IDF allowed huge amounts of humanitarian aid into Gaza. This sort of task is regarded by military tacticians as risky and dangerous at the best of times…' The IDF phoned over 30,000 Palestinian households in Gaza, urging them in Arabic to leave homes where Hamas might have stashed weapons or be preparing to fight… Despite Israel's extraordinary measures, of course innocent civilians were killed and wounded…'

'Israel must be proactive in preventing adverse stories in the media. It must establish 'rapid rebuttal units' which rush to establish the facts and get them to the media. If they are unaware or unsure of the facts they must say so. In addition, Israel must be sure to investigate all mistakes that are made…'[1]

The real 'disproportionate response' is that of the world's media!

NOTES

1. For fuller details go to www.jcpa.org
2. See also Colonel Kemp's recent three minute speech at the United Nations:
http://www.raymondcook.net/blog/index.php/2009/10/19/
colonel-richard-kemp-and-the-truth-about-operation-cast-lead/

Appendix 4

Testimony of Arab/Jewish reconciliation

This is an extract from a testimony of Karen Davis concerning her reconciliation to the Arabs. Karen is a Messianic Jewess who is married to David, an Israeli Pastor. David is not Jewish. They lead Carmel Assembly and this extract is from her account as published on their website.

'... in 1989...my husband David and I moved to Israel, leaving behind the world of the arts in New York City, with a vision from the Lord to help drug addicts through the power of God's love. It was not accidental that it had been through an Arab woman in the Old City of Jerusalem that we first learned of the drug epidemic in Israel. It was also not by chance that our first invitation to minister as a couple in Israel came from a pastor in Turan, an Arab village in Galilee. As we were approaching the village where I would sing and David would preach, I suddenly realized that I felt nothing for the people before whom we were about to minister. I didn't feel hostile or angry, but I realized that my heart was cold toward them. After all, hadn't I come to Israel to reach out to my people- the Jewish people- who were hurting and lost? And weren't the Arabs really our enemies?

I told my husband that we needed to stop the car and pray- that I couldn't stand before them with my heart in this condition. As we began to pray, the words of Jesus from Matthew 5:46-48 suddenly came to my mind: "For if you love those who love you, what reward have you? Do not even the tax collectors do the same? And if you greet your brother only, what do you do more than others? Do not even the tax collectors do so? Therefore you shall be perfect, just as your Father in heaven is perfect."

I knew the Lord was saying to me that He loves the Arab people as much as He loves the Jewish people and that He had called me to this land, first and foremost, as His ambassador, to represent Him and His love here on earth. Even though I was now an Israeli citizen, my true and deepest citizenship was in the kingdom of heaven (Phil. 3:20). He was telling me that in everything I would do here in Israel that He wanted me to carry His heart at all times for both peoples, the Arabs and the Jews. I began to weep as the Spirit of the Lord came into my heart, melting away the coldness, and enlarging and filling it with His love for the Arab people.

We started the car again and drove into the Arab village. As we entered the little church, the Arab women greeted me with open arms and kisses. I stood before them and sang one of my favorite songs, "Behold I'm New in Jesus," thanking God that He enabled me to sing those words "in spirit and in truth."

Some months later we began reaching out to drug addicts in Haifa and founded "Beit Nitzachon" (House of Victory), a residential rehabilitation center for Jews and Arabs. For over a decade now we have witnessed the miracle of the transforming power of God's love as He works in the hearts of afflicted men to be reconciled to Him through the blood of Yeshua and then toward each other.

The Lord has continued the good work He began in my heart that day on the road to Turan. For some time I still found it difficult to hear the Arabic language spoken, as I had usually heard it spoken in anger and for so long associated it with acts of violence toward the Jewish people. Now as I was developing relationships with my Arab brothers and sisters in the Lord and heard their prayers and their worship in Arabic, I began to hear the true beauty of the language when it became a language of love.

I sought out an Arab sister in Haifa, Ibtisam, and asked her to teach me some of her worship songs in Arabic. As the worship leader of Kehilat HaCarmel (the congregation which arose alongside Beit Nitzachon), I now often include an Arabic song in our mostly Hebrew worship services.

The Lord has called us as Jews and Gentiles- Jews and Arabs- into one body (Eph. 2:15-16) in order that we would become a dwelling place of God, a habitation for His Spirit (Eph.2:21). We have sought in our work at Beit Nitzachon and Kehilat HaCarmel to express this unity, in hope that many would glimpse the reality of the kingdom of God- that those who have never known His love would "taste and see" that Yeshua is the "new and living way" to true peace.

Whether or not a political solution is ever found to our situation here, it will only be through the atoning blood of the Lamb of God that we will be delivered from the hostility and pain lodged in our hearts as Jews and Arabs here in the Middle East'.

© Karen Davis www.carmel-assembly.org.il

Chronology of key events since 1896

1896   Theodore Herzl, a Jew, produces his book entitled 'The Jewish State' outlining his vision for a restored Jewish state. He became known as the Father of modern Zionism.

1917   Issue of the 'Balfour Declaration', stating that Britain's government 'view with favour the establishment in Palestine of a national home for the Jewish people'. This was the end of 400 years of Turkish rule of Palestine and beginning of the British administration, known as the 'British Mandate'.

1922   Nearly 80% of Palestine was allocated by the British and designated as 'Transjordan', controlled by the Arabs. Jewish settlement was barred there.

1939   British Prime Minister Neville Chamberlain announces a 'White Paper' stating that an independent Arab state would be created within ten years. Jewish immigration was to be limited to 75,000 for the next five years, after which it was to cease altogether, unless the Arabs consented. Sales of land in most areas to Jews were to be prohibited. The Arabs rejected the proposal.

1939-1945 World War Two including Hitler's 'Final Solution', an attempt to liquidate world Jewry. This attempt is known by the Jews as 'The Shoah' and generally as 'The Holocaust'

1947   On November 29, The United Nations voted to set up both an Arab and a Jewish state in Palestine. The Jews accepted it, but it was rejected by the Arabs.

1948 (14 May) *The 'Declaration of Independence'* was signed and State of Israel was proclaimed.

1948 (15 May) *'War of Independence'* declared on Israel by Egypt, Syria, Transjordan, Lebanon and Iraq. A ceasefire ended it in January 1949.

1967 *'Six Day War'* from 5 to 10 June. Israel responded to aggression from various Arab nations by 'pre-emptive strikes'. The Israelis especially destroyed Egyptian planes. Israel seized Jerusalem from Jordan and parts of territory annexed in 1948 by Jordan called the 'West Bank' (biblically Judea & Samaria). The Temple Mount was left under Islamic control. The Golan Heights were taken from Syria.

1973 *'Yom Kippur' War.* In October, Arab armies from Egypt, Syria, Iraq, Saudi Arabia, Kuwait, Libya, Algeria, Sudan, Morocco and Lebanon attacked Israel on the annual Day of Atonement. Jordan participated to a lesser extent. War lasted for 19 days and took place during the Muslim month of Ramadan.

1982- 1985 *First Lebanon War.* This began on 6 June 1982. The Israel Defence Forces invaded Southern Lebanon after an assassination attempt on Israel's ambassador to the UK. Before that, there had been a series of attacks by the Palestine Liberation Organisation and Israeli reprisals.

1987 *First 'Intifada'.* Arabic for 'shaking off'. Developed into a massive civil resistance campaign in the West Bank and Gaza. It was violent but not, for the most part, involving guns and bombs.

2000 *Second 'Intifada' known as the 'Al-Aqsa Intifada'.* There is a Mosque called 'Al-Aqsa' on the Temple Mount.

This Intifada started allegedly after an unwelcome visit by former Israeli Prime Minister Ariel Sharon to the Temple Mount late in 2000. In fact, it started before the visit. This became Israel's longest war, involving widespread military activities on both sides, lasting at least until 2005.

2005 Israel withdrew from Gaza, evicting thousands of its own citizens and rendering many of them jobless, with their Palestinian employees. The militant Islamist party Hamas now rules Gaza.

2006 *Second Lebanon War.* In reality, a war between Israel and an extremist Islamist faction called 'Hezbollah' (The 'Party of God').

2008 *Operation 'Cast Lead'.* After years of Hamas rockets raining down on Southern Israel, Israel attacks Gaza in an attempt to kill Hamas leaders and to destroy the infrastructure of Hamas.

Glossary

Al-Aqsa Mosque   Grey-domed mosque at the southern end of the Temple Mount (see below). The name means 'the distant one' and it is thought by many Muslims to be the place to which Mohammed took a 'night journey'-i.e in a dream.

Aliyah   Term used to describe Jews from anywhere in the world emigrating to Israel. It comes from a Hebrew word meaning to 'go up'. The last book in the 'Old' Testament in the Jewish Bible is 1 Chronicles, which ends with the phrase '*let him go up!*'

Anti-semitism   I use this term in this book to mean 'anti-Jewish' in accordance with its general, modern use. However, others are quite correct to point out that, strictly-speaking, the term can also mean 'anti-Arab'. They too are a Semitic people, ie descendants of Shem, son of Noah. Earlier in history, it has a wider meaning still.

Arab League   A regional organisation of 22 Arab states in Southwest Asia and North and Northeast Africa.

Christian Zionist   A Christian who understands the events of the twentieth century leading up to the creation of the State of Israel and beyond to be a fulfilment of biblical prophecy and part of God's ongoing purposes with the Jews. Many Christian Zionists seek to practically support Israel.

Church Fathers   The outstanding theologians of the first six centuries AD, such as Origen, Athanasius and Augustine.

Gaza/Gaza Strip   A small strip of land just north of Egypt's Sinai Desert densely populated by more than one million

Palestinian Arabs. It was occupied by Egypt until 1967, when Israel took it in the Six Day War and occupied it until 2005. Hamas (see below) now controls Gaza.

Hamas Arabic word meaning 'zeal' or 'courage' and an acronym for Islamic Resistance Movement. It is a militant Islamist Palestinian Organisation founded in Gaza in 1987 that opposes the existence of the state of Israel.

Intifada Shake off, or uprising.

Islam Submission and obedience to the will of Allah (God). Some commentators suggest a link with the Arabic word *Salaam* meaning peace, but this is doubtful.

Islamist A term which is used to refer to *political* Islam, called by some 'Islamic fundamentalism'. This includes the spreading of Islam throughout the world, including the establishment of full Islamic Republics.

Islamic Republic A country ruled by a Muslim Government and under Islamic law, with non-Muslims being officially second-class citizens

Israeli Arabs Arabs who chose to remain in Israel after 1948 and their descendants. They are citizens of Israel and number around one million out of a total population of about seven million.

Jew I use this term to mean anyone descended from any of the 12 sons of Jacob, in accordance with its common usage. However, the term can mean only those of the tribes of Judah and Benjamin.

Jihad A term with various meanings, its literal meaning being 'striving'. I use it in this book to refer to the obligation on Muslims to spread Islam as an all-encompassing religious, political, economic and social system. This can be by military or ideological means, or both.

Messianic Jew A Jew who believes that Jesus (Yeshua) is the Messiah and Saviour.

Millennium A period of 1000 years yet to come, mentioned frequently in the prophetic books of the Bible, but not given a time frame until Revelation 20.

Mufti One who is competent to give an opinion on a case of Islamic law.

Palestinian Arabs Arabs who live outside of Israel, but used to live there or are descended from those who did, are known as 'Palestinians'.

Palestinian Authority Abbreviated form of 'Palestinian National Authority. The administrative organisation established to govern parts of the Palestinian territories of the West Bank and Gaza Strip. Formed in 1994 as a five year interim body to enable 'final status negotiations' with the government of Israel. However, those negotiations have never been concluded.

Reformers Those who led a wide-ranging movement of spiritual renewal in Europe, occurring primarily in the 16th century, but anticipated by earlier reform initiatives.

Replacement Theology The belief that, when the church came into being, God's purposes with Israel/The Jews as a covenant people came to an end. In this view, their covenants are

147

entirely replaced by the New Covenant. It often takes Bible promises to Israel and says they are now for the church, while leaving the biblical curses to the Jews.

Road Map A three stage plan created in 2003 and backed by the USA, United Nations, European Union and Russia. It aimed to create a Palestinian state by the end of 2008 but failed.

Second Temple The First was built by King Solomon- See 1 Kings. It was destroyed on the ninth of Av, a Hebrew month, by Nebuchadnezzar. It was later rebuilt and much improved by King Herod. It stood from 516 BC to 70 AD, when it was destroyed by the Romans, again on the ninth of Av.

Sharia Law Islamic law in general, but specifically as derived from the Qur'an and other Islamic writings and developed as a system of jurisprudence. The path of duty, both ritual and general, for Muslims. The only rule of government for a true Islamic state.

Temple Mount The elevated area built on top of Mount Moriah in Jerusalem as a support for the Jewish temples. Known by many Muslims as 'The Noble Sanctuary', coupled with a denial that the area has *any* historical Jewish connections at all.

The Great Tribulation Period of seven literal years believed by many Christians to take place in the End Times. A time of severe persecution of Jews. Some Christians believe the church will be 'raptured' before the Tribulation, others believe the church will endure it.

War of Independence See 'Chronology of key events since 1896'.

West Bank An area of the former British-mandated Palestine, west of the Jordan River, and unilaterally annexed by Jordan after the War of Independence. Known biblically as the 'mountains of Judea and Samaria'. Israel captured the area in 1967.

Western Wall The ancient remnant of the Herodian retaining wall on the western side of the Temple Mount platform. It is the focus of Jewish prayer and the only part of the area accessible to Jews, the Temple Mount itself being under Muslim jurisdiction. No part of the original Second Temple remains intact, but its huge stones are still to be found loose in Jerusalem. Known also as 'the Wailing Wall' and each year on the ninth of Av (see 'Second Temple' above) Jews gather to lament the destruction of both temples.

Yeshua The Hebrew word for Jesus, often used by Messianic Jews

Zionist A supporter of the movement to establish an autonomous Jewish national home in Israel and to develop the State of Israel.

Note
The definitions I have included of 'Israeli' and 'Palestinian' Arabs are, of necessity, simplistic. For a broader understanding, more reading must be done on the subject.

Recommended Resources

Books

Bard, Mitchell G, *Myths and Facts, A Guide to the Arab-Israeli Conflict,* American Israeli Cooperative Enterprise 2001, ISBN 097129450X

Bennett, Ramon, *Saga, Israel and the Demise of Nations,* Arm of Salvation 1994, ISBN 9659000030

Brown, Michael L, *Our Hands are Stained with Blood,* Destiny Image Publishers 1992, ISBN 1560430680

Crombie, Kelvin, *For the Love of Zion,* Hodder & Stoughton 1991, ISBN 0340558059.

Davis, David, *The Elijah Legacy,* Thomas Nelson Inc, ISBN 0497210000.

Dixon, Murray, *Israel: The Land of God's Promise,* Sovereign World 2006, ISBN 1852404426

Fisher, Julia, *A Future for Israel?,* Authentic Media, 2006, ISBN 1860245315

Kac, Arthur W, *The Rebirth of the State of Israel, (is it of God or of Men?),* Baker Book House 1976, ISBN 0801053811

Lambert, Lance, *The Uniqueness of Israel,* Kingsway Publications 2002, ISBN 0854765158

Maalouf, Tony, *Arabs in the Shadow of Israel,* Kregel Publications 2003, ISBN 0852431840

Maltz, Steve *The Land of Many Names,* Authentic Lifestyle 2003, ISBN 1860242871

Peters, Joan, *From Time Immemorial,* JKAP Publications USA 1984, ISBN 0963624202

Price, Randall, *Fast Facts on the Middle East Conflict,* Harvest House Publishers 2003, ISBN 0736911421

Price, Randall, *Unholy War; America, Israel & Radical Islam,* Harvest House Publishers, ISBN 0736908234

Prince, Derek, *The Destiny of Israel and the Church,* Word (UK) Ltd 1992, ISBN 085009562X

Prince, Derek, *The Last Word on the Middle East*, Derek Prince Ministries International, ISBN 0310600413

Richards, Rob, *Has God Finished with Israel*, Authentic Lifestyle 2003, ISBN 186024 3576.

Scheller, Gustav, *Operation Exodus*, Sovereign World Limited 1998, ISBN 1852402261

Sookdheo, Patrick, *A Christian's Pocket Guide to Islam*, Isaac Publications 2005, ISBN 1845501195.

Sookdheo, Patrick, *Understanding Islamic Terrorism: The Islamic Doctrine*, Isaac Publications 2004, ISBN 0954783506

Sookdheo, Patrick, *Global Jihad: The Future in the Face of Militant Islam,* Isaac Publications 2007, ISBN 978714121

Sookdheo, Patrick, *Faith, Power and Territory: A Handbook of British Islam*, Isaac Publications 2008, ISBN 09781413X

Sookdheo, Patrick, *Islam: The Challenge to the Church,* Isaac Publications 2008, ISBN 0954783549

Yousef, Mosab Hassan, *Son of Hamas,* Tyndale House Publishers, Inc 2010, ISBN 978-1-4143-3307-6

Booklet

The Mosque and its Role in Society- available online from http://www.ktshop.com/products.asp?recnumber=84

Magazines

Israel Today: A monthly magazine from Jerusalem written by Messianic Jews to a high standard of professional journalism- theological, devotional, political and archaelogical. Short articles and news extracts. They also have footage available online at http://footage.israeltoday.co.il Call 00972 26226881 or go to www.israeltoday.co.il This magazine is very pro-Israel but includes interviews with people who disagree with the views of the regular contributors, sometimes radically.

Sword: A bi-monthly UK magazine 'published to bring the unchanging word of God to the people of God and through them to the nations of the world'. Call 0844 4140618 or go to www.swordpdp.com

Websites (see also 'Christian Organisations':

www.arabsforisrael.com
www.ariel.org
www.jewishvirtuallibrary.org
www.lancelambert.org
www.mideastweb.org
www.palestinefacts.org
www.saltshakers.com
www.shoebat.com
www.snopes.com
www.whyisrael.org
www.palestinianzionistorganisation.com

Christian Organisations

- Bridges For Peace
Tel: 00972 2 624 5004
- Christian Friends of Israel
Tel: 01323 410810 or www.cfi.org.uk
- Chosen People Ministries
Tel: 020 8455 7911 or www.chosenpeople.org.uk
- The Church's Ministry Among Jewish People (CMJ)
Tel: 01623 883960 or www.cmj.org.uk
CMJ Israel: Tel 00972 2 627 7730 or www.cmj-israel.org

- Ebenezer Emergency Fund International (Operation Exodus)
Tel: 01202 294455 or www.operation-exodus.org
- Hatikvah Film Trust
Tel: 0845 2308788 or www.hatikvah.co.uk
- Isrelate www.isrelate.com
- Jews for Jesus
Tel: 020 7267 5597 or www.jewsforjesus.org.uk
- Near East Ministry (for Arabs & Jews)
Tel: 0113 2306 491 or www.neareastministry.com
- Prayer For Israel
Tel: 0870 766 8306 or www.prayer4i.org
- Reshet Ministries*
Tel: 0116 2215094 or www.reshetministries.org.uk
- Streams in the Desert
www.streamsinthedesert.org.uk

* Note

This is based in Leicester, UK, and is led by the author of this book. 'Reshet' means network and it seeks to network with individuals, churches and groups who have an interest in Israel and related teaching. Some of us in Leicester feel that our city has a key role and this may have some connection with its history as mentioned in passing in chapter 6.